YOUNG READERS' EDITION

THANK YOU FOR VOTING

THE PAST, PRESENT, AND FUTURE OF VOTING

by **ERIN GEIGER SMITH**

with **KATHLEEN KRULL**

HARPER

An Imprint of HarperCollinsPublishers

Library of Congress Control Number: 2020933696
ISBN 978-0-06-297238-5

Typography by Laura Mock
20 21 22 23 24   PC/LSCH   10 9 8 7 6 5 4 3 2 1

First Edition

For Reed, my future voter

CONTENTS

NOTE TO THE READER

Welcome to the world of voting. Don't stress: voting is something you already know a lot about. It's something you do all the time—when you're choosing classmates for your student government, when your family is deciding whether to go to the park or watch a movie and everyone says their choice, or when you support your favorite singer on *The Voice*.

The voting we're talking about in this book is about political elections, or when American citizens choose who will hold political office (like the president or mayor), or decide whether their city or state should make certain changes.

The elections you probably hear the most about are

the ones for president of the United States, but those only happen every four years. There are many elections that occur both at the same time and between those. Every two years there are national elections for members of the U.S. House of Representatives and U.S. Senate. Your state governor and legislators are also elected, and so is the mayor of your town, your city council, usually your school board, and sometimes even judges and your local sheriff.

This is a critical kind of voting—it's part of our democracy, the concept that defines America. When people *don't* vote, it's a problem for our democracy and our country. We'll never know what the country truly wants and needs unless more of us participate. The more you vote, the more politicians pay attention to your concerns.

Voting is one of America's greatest sources of pride, but something about it may shock you: many Americans don't vote, even when they're old enough.

THE WISDOM OF FRANKLIN D. ROOSEVELT

"Nobody will ever deprive the American people of the right to vote except the American people themselves—and the only way they could do that is by not voting." So declared Franklin D. Roosevelt, president of the United States from 1933 to 1945, the longest any person has served in that office.

His quote pops up in the news and on social media any time there's an election. It is used to encourage Americans to vote. His words represent the height of patriotism. They remind us that we, as citizens of the United States, have to make our opinions known about issues that affect our country, including education, the economy, the environment, and many other things.

To solve that problem of people not voting—and it is a problem that can be solved—we need to better understand our voting history. In a way, the history of America is the story of how people got the all-important right to vote.

The more you know about voting in elections, the more you can help the country increase the number of people who vote, and the more likely you are to vote yourself. Everyone who studies voting agrees that the person with the best chance of getting certain people to vote—your friends, your parents, your brothers and sisters, even your teachers—is YOU!

The non-voting problem is particularly acute with young people. Each generation, for instance, votes at lower rates than the one older, and at times about a quarter of young adults speak for all young adults. (That's like if one friend out of four always got to make all the choices.)

Roosevelt spoke his words in 1944. But if we look at what was happening at the time, we find that some Americans were being treated very differently from others, and many were being prevented from voting.

Roosevelt knew that, and he talked about it later in the speech: "The right to vote must be open to our citizens [no matter their] race, color or creed . . . The sooner we get to that basis of political equality, the better it will be for the country as a whole."

He was arguing that Americans should be able to vote no matter what color their skin was or what country their family was originally from. He knew the United States had a lot of work to do to make voting fair.

FROM A PERSONAL POINT OF VIEW

I live in New York City and am a journalist. But my own story begins in the tiny town of Liberty, Texas. Its population is now just shy of 10,000 people. It was even smaller when I was growing up. Towering oak trees shade the three-story limestone courthouse in the town square. It's Liberty's seventh courthouse; the first one was built of logs when Texas was still part of Mexico, back in 1831. The town burger spot is across the street, and multiple churches are within walking distance, their steeples among the tallest things in town.

I feel a strong connection to both New York and Texas, but around election time, my hometown and Manhattan seem like different universes. Liberty County voters overwhelmingly choose candidates from the Republican

Party, while my current neighborhood in New York heavily favors Democrats.

VOTING LINGO

Political parties aren't actually parties—they're groups of people with similar thoughts about government. Throughout our history, parties have evolved and come and gone. One of the two major ones now is the Democratic Party (derives from "democracy"), which tends to promote progressive or liberal ideas and wants the government to play a role in protecting citizens' welfare. The 2016 Democratic presidential candidate was Hillary Clinton. The other major party is the Republican Party (from *res publica*, which means "public thing"), which promotes a socially conservative agenda and prefers to limit the role of government. The 2016 Republican presidential candidate was Donald Trump.

Each place has its reasons for supporting different candidates, and that is clear to me. But what is discouraging is that they both fear that they won't be represented, that their wants and needs will be ignored, if their candidate doesn't win. Politicians are public servants; their job is to serve the public's needs. That should include respecting the concerns of *all* the people they represent.

But even if people worry about being represented, and with all the talk of the country's very strong political feelings, so many eligible citizens stay home on Election Day.

They don't vote. And those who do vote can't always pick up the slack for their neighbors.

Every vote does count, but if others who share your views don't vote, the candidate you support has a smaller chance of winning.

This book is itself an attempt to help solve the problem of people not voting. It's divided into three sections. The first explains when different groups of Americans—African Americans, Native Americans, women, and young people, among others—were first allowed to vote. It also looks at current examples of laws that make it more difficult for some people to vote, and ways some states have made it easier. When you read about the fierce struggle of some groups to be able to vote, you'll understand the focus on protecting that right, and will hopefully be inspired to think about new laws affecting it.

The second section explains the importance of educating yourself and provides explanations of mysterious voting topics like gerrymandering and the Electoral College.

The third takes you inside organizations, like *Grown-ish* star Yara Shahidi's, that work to get people to vote, and shows how their actions and attitudes can be followed to get your friends and family excited about voting.

THE IMPORTANCE OF FARMERS

Many elections, including presidential elections, are held on Tuesdays in November—officially the first Tuesday after the first Monday of November.

Why November? In the 1800s, many people were farmers who had to stay home and take care of their crops until growing season was over in the fall. They also couldn't easily travel in winter due to cold and snow. So early November was the best time between work and winter.

Why Tuesdays? It was 1845 when a particular Election Day in the fall was set, and it also had to do with farmers. It couldn't be a Monday, because people didn't travel on Sundays for religious reasons and long trips would require leaving then. Wednesdays, farmers would usually bring their crops to sell at market. So Tuesday it was.

What I'm not doing—*at all*—is telling you who to vote for. I believe the more people who vote, the more representative and responsive our government will be. And we need everyone to vote in every election, not just the presidential ones. As the new coronavirus spread across the country in early 2020, mayors and other city officials made important decisions about how to keep essentials available and protect citizens' lives. No one can afford to sit out those elections. Figuring out the best way to achieve the largest turnout should have nothing to do with one side or the other and everything to do with supporting democracy.

This book is nonpartisan (which means not in favor of any political party), but it is definitely pro-voting.

Roosevelt's campaign speech seventy-five years ago was a plea for voter turnout, and it is just as relevant today. He said we shouldn't "be slackers on registration day or Election Day," and that only a large number of voters could show for sure who the American people really wanted to win. The "health and vigor of our democratic system depends on the public spirit and devotion of its citizens" to expressing themselves at the ballot box, he said.

If we want our country to last, in other words, the public needs to be dedicated to voting. Roosevelt's right. Let's listen to him!

Let's not be slackers. Let's learn all we can about voting and devote ourselves to democracy. I hope you'll vote as soon as you can after you turn eighteen, and that you'll vote in every election in every race on the ballot. And that until then, you'll bring your family and friends and your neighbors and your teachers to the polls.

Thank you for learning about voting.

PART ONE

THE STORIES OF HOW WE GOT THE VOTE

STRUGGLING FOR VOTING EQUALITY

The whole point of a democracy is supposed to be that citizens take an active role in deciding how the country or state or city should be run. They get to vote on it.

Democracies have been around for thousands of years—all the way back to the fifth century BCE, and forms of it even before that! And controversy has always swirled around who can vote.

THE FIRST DEMOCRACY

The first widely known democracy was in Athens, Greece, and all adult citizens were required to participate in governing. The catch: only free men were considered citizens. Women, children, and slaves were not, so they couldn't vote.

In the United States today, with certain exceptions, any citizen who is at least eighteen years old has the right to vote, no matter what race or religion they are, no matter their level of education, no matter how much or little money they have.

But for a very long time, that wasn't the case. Unfair as it was, voting was largely limited to white men who owned land.

In the late 1770s and 1780s, when America was figuring out how it would operate as a new nation separate from England, each state made its own voting rules. This was how it had worked with the colonies before they became states. America continued to mostly copy the way people had voted in England, and that meant voting was a privilege for wealthy, mostly white male landowners.

FOUNDER JOHN ADAMS ON WHO SHOULD VOTE

In 1776, John Adams wrote that if men who had no property were allowed a voting voice, "New claims will arise. Women will demand a vote. Lads from twelve to twenty-one will think their rights not enough attended to, and every man who has not a farthing, will demand an equal voice with any other in all acts of state. It tends to confound and destroy all distinctions, and prostrate all ranks, to one common level."

This quote is cleaned up a little bit for modern punctuation, but to me what Adams is really saying is: we must keep the voting power for ourselves, or people will see they, too, are entitled to it in a true democracy. Everyone would be equal! The nightmare!

But many new Americans took democracy seriously, and eventually, laws were proposed to make voting more fair. Different laws affected different groups, so one way to examine the history of voting in the United States is to look at how groups of people—African Americans, Native Americans, immigrants (those who come to live in the United States from another country), eighteen-year-olds, and women—were victorious in getting the right to vote.

VICTORIES IN VOTING:
More Recent Than You Think

The dates of those voting rights victories—court decisions or new laws that granted certain people the right to vote—can sound like ancient history. But groundbreaking voting laws have benefited the parents and grandparents of today's Americans. My great-grandmother Hazel was born in 1900, and would have been among the first women able to vote nationwide as soon as she turned twenty-one. Many immigrants of Asian descent born that same year wouldn't be eligible for U.S. citizenship until the year they turned fifty-two. An African American born at the turn of the twentieth century and living in the South may not have cast a ballot on Election Day until she was sixty-five years old.

THE VERY FIRST VOTE FOR PRESIDENT

Before 1787, the country was governed by a document called the Articles of Confederation, which left most of the power to the states and didn't create a position for a powerful president. Once America won the Revolutionary War and declared independence from England, the need for a national, or federal, government became pressing. Then came a time of great debate—the 1787 Constitutional Convention, which took place in Philadelphia over five months. It gave us the U.S. Constitution, the document that still governs us today.

The new Constitution provided for a president, and the first vote took place in 1789. The outcome couldn't have been more predictable—General George Washington, a hero of the Revolutionary War, won.

Actually, it was "electors" from the states who elected Washington. Just as in today's presidential elections, the president was officially selected by the Electoral College. (More about this mysterious Electoral College in Part Two.)

Today, a popular vote is held in each state and voters vote for who they would like to win. They essentially tell the electors who to vote for. In the 1789 election, however, states chose the electors and had different ways of doing it—some states did let citizens vote for them, but some were appointed by the state legislatures.

In that particular election, George Washington received *all* the electoral votes; he's the only president who's ever been elected unanimously. (It was a lot easier to do that when it was only a few electors voting and not the whole country weighing in.)

Just as presidential elections went from being a fairly predictable event to the years-long campaigns we see now, who could vote in those elections has also changed a lot.

Adams's prediction that citizens would eventually demand one of the most important rights of citizenship—voting—was correct. Americans learned to use their voices to argue for their rights, and use the words in the Constitution to argue that equal should mean equal for *everyone*.

As the nation grew, women, African Americans, Native Americans, and immigrants were among the groups that would have to overcome discrimination, skeptical politicians, physical attacks, and court battles to secure their right to vote.

AFRICAN AMERICANS AND THE VOTE

African Americans have been treated poorly throughout America's voting history. Politicians at every level of government repeatedly and purposefully discriminated against African Americans. Denying them the right to vote has been a focus of that prejudice. If you don't get to vote, it's difficult to change the unfair laws holding you back.

Many African Americans were enslaved until 1865, when the Civil War between the Northern and Southern states ended. At the end of that year, the Thirteenth Amendment to the Constitution, which said "neither slavery nor involuntary servitude . . . shall exist," was adopted by the states.

Even though slavery was abolished, the right of African Americans to vote would continue to be a topic of controversy and legal disputes for years to come. That is true even though free African American men had sometimes been allowed to vote even before the Civil War. Even when John Adams was making his proclamations about voting, in 1776, there were exceptions to the rule that only white men could vote.

SOMETIMES BLACK MEN HAD THE RIGHT TO VOTE. AND SOMETIMES IT WAS TAKEN AWAY.

Every state—even today—has its own constitution. The laws in those constitutions can't go against anything in the U.S. Constitution, but they can add details or new requirements. In New Jersey, for about thirty years starting in 1776, property-owning women and free black men could vote. That ended in 1807, when the state legislature limited voting to white, property-owning men. In 1777, Vermont's constitution abolished slavery for men over twenty-one and gave those males the right to vote. Pennsylvania is another state that did allow free black men to vote, but changed their laws in 1838 to allow only whites to vote.

FIGHTING BACK: ROBERT PURVIS

Robert Purvis was born in 1810 to a free black woman and a white cotton merchant. When Purvis's father died in 1826, he left him a lot of money. Purvis became an antislavery activist, and was the first African American member of the Pennsylvania Abolition Society. When Pennsylvania was considering taking away free African American men's right to vote in 1838, Purvis made a reasoned and heartfelt argument in a document called *Appeal of Forty Thousand Citizens, Threatened with Disfranchisement.* ("Disfranchisement" meaning taking away a person's right to vote.) He pointed out free black men had been voting in Pennsylvania for a half century, and how important the right to vote was to citizens. When you take away an individual's right to vote, he said, you have given the government full power over him, and have made the government a little worse for everyone else, too.

When the Civil War began in 1861, only a handful of states allowed black men to vote equal to whites under their own state laws. But black men fought in the Civil War in great numbers—around 180,000 in the Union Army—and began pushing for equality in all states, including voting rights, as the war came to an end.

In 1865, for instance, a group of fifty-nine African Americans from Tennessee presented a petition to a pro-Union convention in Nashville, asking for the right to vote and referring to those still fighting in the war. That same year, black citizens of New Orleans organized a mock (pretend) election to show how seriously they took the right to vote.

THE FOURTEENTH AND FIFTEENTH AMENDMENTS TO THE CONSTITUTION

Increased pressure to allow African Americans to vote eventually led to the Fourteenth and Fifteenth Amendments. The Fourteenth Amendment, passed by Congress in 1866 and agreed to by the states in 1868, granted citizenship to all people born or naturalized in the United States, and guaranteed all citizens "equal protection of the laws." It also aimed to force Southern states to allow black men to vote by threatening to reduce their number of members in the U.S. House of Representatives if they didn't. Essentially, if they didn't allow black men to vote, these states would have less of a say in national politics.

WHAT DOES IT TAKE TO CHANGE THE CONSTITUTION?

A change to the Constitution is called an amendment, and it usually means something is added to recognize a right. Amendments are rare and difficult to get done. The Constitution provides a few ways to do it, but most amendments to the Constitution have been passed this way:

- Both the U.S. Senate and U.S. House must approve the language of the amendment; in order to pass, two-thirds of the Senate and the same percentage of the U.S. House must approve.

- After the two houses of Congress approve, the amendment goes to the states to decide.

- Three-fourths of states, via their state legislatures, must approve the amendment.

- If enough states approve, the amendment is "ratified" and made part of the Constitution.

Additional laws called the Reconstruction Acts—part of the effort to put the country back together after the Civil War—had even stronger language, saying that in order for Southern states to be let back into the United States, they had to approve the Fourteenth Amendment and write new state constitutions that allowed black males the right to vote. By July 1868, seven states had been readmitted. Historian and Harvard professor Alexander Keyssar wrote: "Black enthusiasm for political participation was so great the freedmen often put down their tools and [stopped] working when elections or conventions were being held."

HIGHLIGHTS FOR AFRICAN AMERICANS DURING THE RECONSTRUCTION ERA (1865–1877)

During Reconstruction, an estimated 2,000 black men held elective office.

1868 One house (the lower house of the General Assembly) in South Carolina's state legislature was majority black.

1870 Hiram Revels took his oath of office as a U.S. senator for Mississippi, the first African American to hold an office in the U.S. Congress.

1870 Joseph Rainey of South Carolina became the first African American member of the U.S. House of Representatives.

NEED FOR THE FIFTEENTH AMENDMENT

Even as Reconstruction was helping African Americans gain political rights and hold offices, many people were fighting to stop the progress. African Americans faced violence in the South, and support for their rights in the North was uneven.

People who wanted African Americans to have voting rights said the Fourteenth Amendment wasn't enough, and that there needed to be another amendment specifically about voting.

So, in 1870, the Fifteenth Amendment was approved by the states. It said that the right to vote "shall not be denied or abridged by the United States or by any State on account of race, color, or previous condition of servitude."

The precise wording of the Fifteenth Amendment was heavily debated, and in the end didn't protect voting rights as some lawmakers wanted. Some had suggested wording that would have outlawed the exact types of discrimination that would end up keeping many African Americans and other minority groups from voting for decades after. And that's despite the fact that the Fifteenth Amendment specifically gave them the right to vote.

Lawmakers decided not to forbid laws and policies designed to keep people from voting if they couldn't read or were of a certain religion or from a certain place. Because the Fifteenth Amendment didn't have that language, many states and the United States government were able to make laws that would keep not just some African Americans, but also Native Americans, Irish people, Hispanics, and Chinese people from voting.

It seemed as though more than just constitutional amendments would be needed to push for fairness.

WHY DID RECONSTRUCTION END?

The end of the Reconstruction Era came shortly after the controversial presidential election of 1876. Samuel Tilden won the popular vote for president. But there was a dispute over

Electoral College votes, and a compromise made Tilden's opponent, Rutherford B. Hayes, the president. The compromise also required the U.S. government to pull its military troops out of the South. With the troops gone, politicians in the South who wanted to limit the rights of black Americans had their chance to do it.

JIM CROW LAWS

From the end of Reconstruction in the late 1870s all the way to the 1960s, there were laws that made it very hard for black people to vote. These were known as "Jim Crow" laws.

WHO WAS JIM CROW?

We know Jim Crow laws enforced racial segregation and discriminated against African Americans, such as requiring separate water fountains for white people and black people, and enforcing poll taxes that kept black people from voting. The term "Jim Crow" is used to describe laws with racist purposes to this day. But who was Jim Crow?

He wasn't a real person, but a character played by a white actor named Thomas Dartmouth "Daddy" Rice in the 1830s. Rice wore blackface and shabby clothes, used an offensive dialect attributed to African Americans, and portrayed the character as dumb. He is said to have based it on a black man (some say a child) he saw singing a song called "Jump Jim Crow" in Louisville, Kentucky. The act was a hit with white people.

It's unclear exactly how the name came to describe the

25

A Florida law in the late 1880s, for example, had separate ballots for different political races and required voters to place the ballot for each race in the correct box, or their vote wouldn't count. But those who couldn't read the box labels had little chance of getting it right. Over the next several years, African American voter turnout in the state dropped from 62 percent to 11 percent.

Another method was the "grandfather clause"—people who didn't own property or couldn't read could vote only if their fathers or grandfathers could vote in 1867. Many black people did not own property and had also not been provided a proper education, so they couldn't read. Their fathers and grandfathers may have been enslaved in the early 1860s, and the Fourteenth and Fifteenth Amendments guaranteeing citizenship to former slaves born in the United States and guaranteeing their right to vote were not made part of the Constitution until after 1867. In 1896, about 130,000 black residents were registered to vote in Louisiana; by 1900, two years after the state enacted its "grandfather clause," the number of

African American voters decreased to around 5,300, and by 1904 only 1,300 African American Louisianans were registered.

By 1940, only 3 percent of eligible African American Southerners were registered to vote due to Jim Crow laws like poll taxes, which required people to pay a fee to vote, and literacy tests. It would take until 1965 before African Americans' right to vote was protected nationwide in any real way.

WHAT WERE LITERACY TESTS?

Literacy tests went way beyond just finding out if someone could read a ballot. They tested knowledge on U.S. or state laws, and sometimes just asked questions that were like puzzles. They weren't given to everyone who tried to vote—just to people, mostly minorities, who officials wanted to keep from voting.

Often if a person got one answer wrong, they "failed" the entire test. The tests were so hard that even educated people today—lawyers, doctors, teachers—would have a tough time passing them. Here are some examples of questions that might have been on a literacy test:

• Name the attorney general of the United States.

• Who pays members of Congress for their services, their home states or the United States?

• At what time of day on January 20 each four years does the term of the president of the United States end?

THE VOTING RIGHTS ACT

Jim Crow laws were just a fact of life, if a very unfair one, for many African Americans until the passage of the 1965 Voting Rights Act (VRA). But the VRA might never have happened without the country seeing and reacting to a violent March day in Alabama.

Even though a civil rights group called the Student Nonviolent Coordinating Committee (SNCC) spent two years working to register African Americans to vote in and around Selma, Alabama, only 335 of the county's 15,000 eligible African American citizens were registered in 1965. The SNCC helped organize a march from Selma to Montgomery, Alabama, for March 7, 1965, to protest the shooting death by a state trooper of twenty-six-year-old civil rights activist Jimmie Lee Jackson.

John Lewis is now known as one of the longest-serving U.S. congressmen and a civil rights legend, but that morning he was a well-known twenty-five-year-old activist carrying a backpack with fruit, a toothbrush, and two books.

Shortly after the march began, a police officer fractured Lewis's skull with a club. On what became known as Bloody Sunday, Lewis was only one of many injured. Images of the clash were all over television, the nation reacted in horror, and the president, Lyndon Johnson, acted quickly to pass voting rights laws that people couldn't find tricks to get around.

Just eight days after Bloody Sunday, Johnson addressed a joint session of Congress. "Many of the issues of civil rights are very complex and most difficult," he said. "But about this there can and should be no argument. Every American citizen must have an equal right to vote."

Johnson's statement led to lawmakers passing the Voting Rights Act, which was signed into law in August 1965. It reinforced the Fifteenth Amendment's requirement that the vote cannot be denied on the basis of race. It, and its later updates, outlawed tactics used to keep black people and members of other minority groups from voting. It also said that states and counties with a history of denying black people or other minority groups the vote couldn't change their voting laws without approval. So, if they tried new tricks, in other words, the federal government could stop them.

WHAT IMPACT DID THE VOTING RIGHTS ACT HAVE?

- By the end of 1965: 250,000 African Americans had newly registered to vote.

- By the end of 1966: nine of thirteen Southern states had 50 percent or more of their eligible African Americans registered.

- By the end of 1967, African American registration in Mississippi had jumped from just 6.7 percent before the VRA to 59.8 percent after.

FIGHTING BACK: ARDIES MAULDIN

Ardies Mauldin was a nurse in her fifties when the Voting Rights Act was passed. Her teenage son, Charles, walked behind Lewis in the Selma march. She had tried to register to vote twice before the passage of the VRA but had not been allowed to.

After it became law, Mauldin went to register to vote in Selma and was able to get through the process quickly. "It didn't take but a few minutes," she said. "I don't know why it couldn't have been like that in the first place."

The Voting Rights Act was renewed, strengthened, and extended multiple times by presidents and lawmakers of both parties, including Barack Obama.

In the years after its passage, the Supreme Court would repeatedly uphold or clarify the VRA's reach and rule against laws that stifled the minority vote. The U.S. Supreme Court, for instance, struck down New York's English-language literacy test in 1966; the law was apparently created to keep Spanish-speaking Puerto Ricans from voting.

Still, efforts to roll the VRA back and make it less effective persisted for decades, including crafting ways of electing local officials that would keep black people and other minority groups from being elected to some local and state offices.

But the Voting Rights Act made access to the polls the true and enforceable law of the land; it allowed citizens who believed their voting rights were being violated to bring challenges in court. This, plus the Fourteenth and Fifteenth Amendments, are used to this day to fight tactics that affect minority voters.

NATIVE AMERICANS AND THE VOTE

To be able to vote, you need to be an American citizen.

This was the rule used to deny rights to Native Americans decade after decade.

Millions of people were already living on the land that would become the United States well before the colonists arrived. The framers of the U.S. Constitution wrote that these indigenous people would be treated as foreigners, not tax-paying citizens—"Indians not taxed." They were excluded from the population count when deciding how many seats in the U.S. House of Representatives each state gets. The Constitution said Congress would oversee commerce (basically buying and selling and other business dealings) with Native Americans and Native Nations in the same way they did other foreign nations.

That might have been fair if the United States had respected Native Nations' independence. But over the next one hundred years, the new country expanded west, forcefully taking over the land of the Native Nations and trying to insist the indigenous people follow American laws.

The arguments made to deny Native Americans citizenship and the vote were a mix of racism and fear. Lawmakers in the 1860s said that indigenous people were an inferior race, and that so many Native Americans lived in areas in what became the Western part of the United States that, if given the right to vote, they could take power.

Disagreement over whether they could be citizens went on for decades. In 1887, a harsh law called the Dawes Act "divided up reservation lands into individual land holdings for tribal members and then sold off the remainder to white settlers," the book *Native Vote* explains. The law also said Native Americans "born within the territorial limits of the United States" could become citizens, but only if they chose to live "separate and apart from any tribe" and adopted the habits of a "civilized" life—in other words, adopting the culture of white people. That would mean giving up their community and their own culture.

A 1924 law, the Indian Citizenship Act, finally allowed Native Americans to become citizens even if they didn't give up their cultural identity or membership, but that somehow didn't solve the voting question once and for all. The U.S. Department of the Interior, which was in charge of the country's relations with the Native Nations, said it meant they could vote. But the governments of states in the West, where Native Americans lived in large numbers, said they couldn't.

Years later, many Native Americans fought in World War II, which gripped the United States from 1941 to 1945. The veterans who came home became an active force in advocating for their people to have the right to vote.

FIGHTING BACK: MIGUEL TRUJILLO

In 1948, war veteran, teacher, and master's degree candidate Miguel Trujillo was told he couldn't vote in New Mexico because that state still barred "Indians not taxed" from voting. People who lived on reservations, as Trujillo did, did not pay property taxes. But he paid plenty of other taxes, including sales tax on things he bought and income tax on money he earned. Trujillo sued the government, saying the "Indians not taxed" rule was unfair.

The New Mexico court agreed with Trujillo. The court said such a law was unconstitutional racial discrimination.

After the victory, Trujillo continued his life as an educator, and went on to fight for immigrant workers and black Southerners suffering under Jim Crow laws. His son, Dr. Michael Trujillo, served as the director of Indian Health Service in President Bill Clinton's administration.

Into the 1950s, Native Americans voted in large enough numbers to decide elections in some Western state elections, but some still couldn't vote at all.

In 1956, the Utah Supreme Court upheld a law that prohibited Indians living on reservations from voting. The court opinion gave reasons including that those who lived on reservations enjoyed government benefits without paying equal taxes. The state legislature repealed the law the next year.

The Voting Rights Act of 1965, besides helping African Americans, also helped make sure Native Americans were not discriminated against. Citizens can file lawsuits when they aren't being treated fairly under the law. Over the years, Native Americans have sued over the lack of polling places on reservations and other discriminatory procedures.

In recent years, some state laws continue to make it difficult. A law in North Dakota required voters to show an ID with an address in order to vote in the 2018 midterms. But some reservations don't have typical street addresses like in other American neighborhoods. Tribal officials had to rush to figure out a way to help those on reservations be able to vote.

IMMIGRANTS AND THE VOTE

Immigrants have been a part of the American story since its very beginning. People who come to live in the United States from another country have strengthened the nation in ways too numerous to count, including the development of the country's culture, its intellectual strength, and even the physical work of building the nation's roads and railroads.

At the same time, there is always some portion of Americans who fear them. Will these new arrivals take jobs, or bring disease, or change who has the power to make laws and decisions? Each time a new immigrant group has grown in large numbers in the country, changes to citizenship law have been debated and very often enacted.

At first, gaining citizenship was straightforward. The Naturalization Act of 1790 said that anyone from another country, if they were of "good moral character," white, and not enslaved, was eligible to become a citizen after living in the United States for two years.

But a mere twenty-five years after the nation's founding, states began to add citizenship requirements to their constitutions to protect power from shifting to voters who were born somewhere else.

As the nation developed in the mid-1800s, the welcome extended to immigrants often depended on how much space and land was available. Farming states like Minnesota, Michigan, Indiana, and Kansas encouraged immigrants to move there and offered them the privilege of voting even before they became citizens.

But in cities, as the numbers of immigrants grew, efforts to limit their rights grew as well. In 1840, New York passed a restrictive voter registration law that affected New York City and its surrounding county, which had a large immigrant population. Into the mid-1850s, as the number of immigrants from Ireland and elsewhere grew in cities, the idea of looking out only for people who were born here began to gain popularity.

WHO WERE THE KNOW-NOTHINGS?

In the 1850s, an anti-immigrant group called the "Know-Nothings" became prominent in the Northeast and parts of the Midwest and South. They started as a secret group, and the name came from critics who would ask people they thought were members of the nativist organization about the group's activities and be told, "I know nothing."

Know-Nothings proudly took on the name and tried to get laws passed, like a *twenty-one-year* waiting period to become a citizen. They also argued for literacy tests meant to keep immigrants from being able to vote even where they were eligible.

Though the Know-Nothings were never able to change U.S. voting laws, they shocked many people by winning governors' races in multiple states, many seats in state governments, and even seats in Congress.

Chinese immigrants were among those targeted for their ethnicity. Anti-Chinese sentiment in California led cities and the state to create money-related hurdles for Chinese businessmen and to try to limit immigration by laborers. A provision in the 1879 California constitution sought to permanently bar natives of China from voting.

Immigrants were dealt a nationwide blow in 1882, when the Chinese Exclusion Act put a hold on immigration from China and made it illegal for Chinese people to become citizens, which also meant no voting rights.

These laws stayed in place until 1943, when China was

a U.S. ally in World War II. Only then were the immigration laws relaxed somewhat—though severe limits still existed—and some Chinese immigrants given the opportunity for citizenship. It wasn't until the next decade that the Immigration and Nationality Act of 1952 gave some Japanese and other Asian immigrants the right to become citizens and earn the right to vote, even though that law also kept a controversial quota system in place.

HOW ASIAN AMERICANS VOTE NOW

When groups of people are kept from voting, it often takes a long time for them to catch up and make voting a habit. The number of Asian Americans who vote still lags behind those of white and black Americans—65 percent of eligible white Americans and 60 percent of black Americans voted in 2016; only half of eligible Asian Americans did.

But that imbalance is changing. In the 2018 election, only about 40 percent of Asian Americans voted, but that was 13 percent higher than the 2014 election. (Presidential elections always have significantly higher turnout than midterm years, so that's why experts compare midterm year to midterm year, and presidential year to presidential year.) Candidates are finally beginning to conduct real outreach to Asian Americans.

EIGHTEEN-YEAR-OLDS AND THE VOTE

Despite all the changes to voting laws we've been talking about, one thing stayed the same: a person had to reach the age of twenty-one before they could vote in the United States. And that restriction stayed in place until the summer of 1971. What happened in 1971 was several decades in the making.

Back in 1942, the draft age had been lowered to eighteen to have more men to fight in World War II. The draft meant young men could be required to join the military, even if they didn't want to. A constitutional amendment to lower the voting age was then introduced under the idea that if you were old enough for military service, you were old enough to vote. The National Education Association also argued that because more people than ever were graduating from high school, eighteen-year-olds were fully prepared for civic life.

But the amendment didn't pass, and the debate over lowering the voting age continued until the Vietnam War. That war had much less popular support than World War II. Young men were being drafted to fight in a war many of them strongly disagreed with, and in the late 1960s there were huge protests across the nation. Many young people believed the country wouldn't even be at war if eighteen- to twenty-year-olds could express their political positions through voting.

In 1970, Senator Edward Kennedy of Massachusetts and two of his colleagues surprised their fellow lawmakers by adding language to lower the voting age to eighteen in a bill extending the Voting Rights Act. The House of Representatives supported the bill—reluctantly—in order to make sure the VRA extension passed.

In a decision later that year, the U.S. Supreme Court ruled that Congress could lower the voting age only for federal elections. (Federal elections are for national government positions, like congress or the president.) It would have meant eighteen-year-olds could vote for those races, but not for governor of their state. The confusion would have made Election Day a real mess.

It seemed like an amendment to the Constitution would be necessary. To succeed, both the Senate and House had to approve the change by a two-thirds vote, and three-fourths of states had to agree as well. The process is so uphill that to date, the Constitution has only twenty-seven amendments—out of many thousands proposed.

With a speed that might be hard to imagine today, lawmakers moved to add the amendment to make the voting age eighteen. The Senate approved it in March 1971, with no senator voting against it. The House quickly approved it as well. By July, enough states had approved, officially making it the Twenty-Sixth Amendment to the Constitution. It was the fastest ratification process in the history of the country.

Roughly four million people turn eighteen every year and become eligible to vote in the United States. Now all we need to do is get them all to do it!

SUFFERING FOR WOMEN'S SUFFRAGE

Not until 1920, nearly 150 years after the founding of the nation, was the Nineteenth Amendment passed, giving women the right to vote in every state. We need to acknowledge how long and arduous women's fight for the vote was, how many complicated and heroic women it took to get it done, and that even with the amendment, black women and other minority women still had work ahead of them to be able to vote.

ABIGAIL ADAMS: AMERICAN HEROINE

As with many hard-fought battles in American history, the right thing to do—treat women as equals—was a topic of conversation right from the start.

In 1776, John Adams and his fellow founders were preparing to write the laws of what would become the United States of America. His wife, Abigail Adams, wrote to him and asked that they think about women's rights as they took on that task:

> I long to hear that you have declared an independency [from Britain]—and by the way in the new . . . laws which I suppose it will be necessary for you to make I desire you would remember the ladies. . . . If particular care and attention is not paid to the ladies we are determined to [stir up] a rebellion, and will not hold ourselves bound by any laws in which we have no voice, or representation.

The grammar and punctuation are made modern here, but what Abigail Adams was saying is clear: I hope the new laws of the United States give women more rights, and if they don't, women may just decide to ignore them.

John Adams understood what she meant. He thought she was funny and a little bold, and said women being upset about their rights was new information to him! But he had no plans to give women rights. "Depend upon it, we know better than to repeal our Masculine systems."

He did soften that by saying men were only powerful in theory, but he didn't seriously entertain her request. Remember the ladies, indeed!

WHERE WOMEN WERE VOTING

Just as with African Americans, there were actually some places women could vote even when the country was brand-new, including:

New Jersey: The state gave women the right to vote until 1807, when the law was changed to allow only white men to vote.

Kentucky: In 1838, women could vote on school-related issues.

Why could women vote in those races and not everything else? It had to do with how women were seen—mostly as mothers and caretakers.

OVER TEA, A MOVEMENT IS BORN

The story of the Nineteenth Amendment actually began seventy years before it became official. It started with the fight to end slavery. People who believed slavery should end were called abolitionists, and some women who were abolitionists gave speeches and talks. Participating in that public way made many of them think of their own rights—shouldn't women have them, too?

One Sunday in July 1848, the idea for a women's rights convention was born when thirty-two-year-old abolitionist Elizabeth Cady Stanton and a few other like-minded women got together at the mansion of Jane Hunt near Seneca Falls, New York. (Hunt had a two-week-old baby at the time!)

A notice soon appeared in the local newspaper inviting others to attend and discuss the "Civil and Political Rights of Women."

The 1848 Seneca Falls Convention in upstate New York is widely considered the kickoff of the women's suffrage movement, even though women's rights events, including African American women fighting to abolish slavery, preceded it.

Around 300 attended the convention on July 19 and 20; men were asked not to join until the second day. The convention's "Declaration of Sentiments"—their list of ideas and concerns—included a number of resolutions and proclaimed "that it is the duty of the women of this country to secure to themselves their sacred right to the elective franchise."

In other words: it's women's duty to make sure they get the right to vote.

THE MAN OF THE MOVEMENT

Frederick Douglass, who had escaped slavery to become a leader in the abolitionist movement, was well-known as a very gifted public speaker. He's credited with encouraging the women at Seneca Falls to include voting rights as one of their goals—believe it or not, some women didn't at first think it was important.

Douglass would become a lifelong advocate for women's suffrage. Preventing women from voting, he said, rejected the importance of "one-half of the moral and intellectual power" of the world.

AFTER SENECA FALLS

After the Seneca Falls event, conventions on women's rights and voting took place in different parts of the country, and well-known activists would speak. Sojourner Truth, who had escaped slavery to became one of the most prominent advocates for human rights, is said to have delivered her famous "Ain't I a Woman" speech at the 1851 Women's Right's Convention in Akron, Ohio:

> *That man over there says that women need to be helped into carriages, . . . and to have the best place everywhere. Nobody ever helps me into carriages, or over mud-puddles, or gives me any best place! And ain't I a woman? Look at me! Look at my arm! I have ploughed and planted. . . . And ain't I a woman?*

(Historians debate whether she spoke those words, but descriptions provided shortly after say—whatever exact words she used—she spoke eloquently about women's rights.) She also spoke memorable words at New York City's 1853 convention, where the large crowd included hecklers repeatedly interrupting the speakers. Truth got the last word to those jeering her. "We'll have our rights; see if we don't. . . . You may hiss as much as you like, but it is comin'."

The conventions continued until the Civil War between Northern and Southern states from 1861 to 1865 put women's rights on hold. The country's war interests came first. Women activists hoped, as had African Americans, that supporting the country in the war efforts might bring more rights when the war ended.

Stanton and Anthony held a meeting in New York City in May 1863 and pledged to drive support for U.S. government action to end slavery, eventually gathering hundreds of thousands of signatures. Their formal organization, the Women's Loyal National League, set up offices in Cooper Union in Manhattan.

BREAKUPS, SHAKE-UPS, AND DISCRIMINATION

After the Civil War, many women were discouraged and angry to see African American (male) rights get more attention than women's rights. As the Fourteenth Amendment was debated—it passed Congress in 1866 and said states would be punished if male citizens weren't allowed to vote—women including Anthony and Stanton felt like women's right to vote should have been a larger part of the discussion. The women were especially angry when the president of the American Anti-Slavery Society urged fighting one battle at a time, saying it was "the Negro's hour."

Some women lashed out. Anthony said that not allowing women to vote was as unfair, and maybe even as cruel, as slavery. Stanton strongly disagreed that certain men's rights should be prioritized over women's, and suggested in harsh language that immigrant and African American men wouldn't know enough to use the right to vote wisely.

Douglass stayed true to his support of women's right to vote, though he made his feelings clear in a speech in 1869, pointing out the differences between the experiences of white women and black people: "When women, because they are women, are hunted down through the cities of New York and New Orleans . . . when their children are not allowed to enter schools; then they will have an urgency to obtain the ballot equal to our own."

Opinions like Stanton's drove a wedge into the women's suffrage community. So in 1869, Stanton and Anthony created a new organization to focus exclusively on women's right to vote, called the National Woman Suffrage Association.

RACISM AND THE WOMEN'S RIGHTS MOVEMENT

Black women participated in the meetings and conventions, including Truth and Mary Church Terrell, cofounder of the National Association of Colored Women. Anthony and prominent anti-lynching activist Ida B. Wells-Barnett at times worked well together, but clashed over Anthony's willingness to put up with the racist prejudices of some Southerners. Suffragists sometimes worked with white Southern women who wanted the vote for white women but did not want African American men *or* women to be able to vote.

Anthony even asked Douglass to sit out the Atlanta women's suffrage convention in 1895. She told Wells-Barnett that she worried that seeing a black man sit with white women on the platform would be too upsetting for Southerners.

But Douglass didn't live to see that convention. He would spend his last day, February 20, 1895, at an earlier women's rights meeting of the National Council of Women in Washington, D.C., where he sat onstage with Anthony. He collapsed that evening while telling his wife about the events of the day. He was seventy-seven.

TENSIONS STILL: THE NEW YORK CITY SUFFRAGE STATUE

In August 2020, a statue of Susan B. Anthony, Elizabeth Cady Stanton, and Sojourner Truth is scheduled to be unveiled in New York City's Central Park to mark the one hundredth anniversary of the women's suffrage amendment.

As first designed, the statue featured only Anthony and Stanton. Many people were concerned that the sculpture didn't recognize the work of the African American women of the movement, so the sculptor added Truth. It will be the first statue of real women in Central Park.

Disagreements between groups of suffragists were ongoing. But so was the slow march toward women's suffrage.

THE "RIGHT" TO VOTE IS ALREADY RIGHT THERE

In the 1870s, women adopted a legal theory promoted by Victoria Woodhull. Way ahead of her time, Woodhull was the first woman to petition Congress in person and the first woman to run for president. (Frederick Douglass was selected as her running mate, though he never actually agreed to it.) Woodhull argued that because the language of the Constitution said citizens could vote, women who were U.S. citizens already had the right. There didn't need to be any changes in the law because the law already said citizens could vote.

During that time period, women were still traveling the country to spread the word about suffrage. Susan B. Anthony's diary on January 1, 1872, described the work she'd done for women's suffrage the year before: she'd traveled some 13,000 miles, state to state, and attended 170 meetings. It was a time when travel was mostly by train and took much longer than it does today.

Also in 1872, women in states including Michigan, New Jersey, and New Hampshire attempted to register and vote, and Anthony herself led what the *New York Times* called a "little band of nine ladies" to the polls. A poll worker challenged Anthony but let her vote when he couldn't think of any legal reason to forbid it. "Well I have been & gone & done it," she wrote to Stanton.

She was soon informed she would be arrested. She insisted the authorities come and handcuff her. She was eventually convicted and fined $100, immediately announcing she would never pay. She didn't.

The argument that women already had the right to vote didn't work right away, so suffragists kept pushing their other ideas. In 1878, Senator Aaron Sargent of California, husband of leading suffragist Ellen Clark Sargent, introduced to Congress what became known as the Susan B. Anthony Amendment. It proposed to change the Constitution to say that women could vote. It took nine more years before the Senate even voted on it, and it lost by a lot.

THE WESTERN STATES

As is still true today with many parts of election law, states were free to set many of their own rules. That meant some of the early wins for women's suffrage came at the state level or even when they were "territories" in the American West:

Wyoming: Sparsely populated Wyoming granted women the right to vote in 1869 when it was still a territory. Why? One possible reason was to encourage women to move there. Women kept their voting rights when Wyoming became a state in 1890.

Utah: Women first had the right to vote in 1870, but a later policy took the right away. The women fought back, setting up women's suffrage organizations in most counties, and made sure that women's suffrage was included when Utah wrote a new constitution to become an official state in 1896.

Colorado: In 1893, Colorado became the first state to approve women's right to vote by a statewide vote. Women suffrage leaders in the state gave lectures, supported leadership that included African American women, and built support from farmers and miners who had a lot of power in the state.

In 1890, the two suffrage organizations ended their rivalries and joined as one, the National American Woman Suffrage Association (NAWSA). This would be the group that would spearhead the way to women's suffrage.

WOMEN WHO DIDN'T WANT WOMEN TO VOTE

For a long time, the majority of people—oddly enough including women—didn't support giving women the vote. Some men and women feared that if women got the vote, they would vote to outlaw alcohol. Men who drank too much were often abusive or unable to hold jobs, and women married to them had no way to protect or defend themselves. It was difficult for women to find work, married women couldn't control their own money or household finances, and husbands were not arrested if they abused their wives. Many connected the suffrage movement with the "prohibition" movement: "We want our beer, and the men do the voting," read one anti-suffrage sign. (Alcohol *was* outlawed in the United States starting in 1920, but the move was unpopular and the ban ended in 1933.)

Arguments against women voting went beyond alcohol, of course—race and class were major factors. Some Southerners were concerned that granting women the right to vote would mean they had to allow black women to vote, and the aggressive tactics used against black men might anger the public if used on a woman. A Mississippi senator was heard to say, "We are not afraid" to hurt a black man, but women can't be treated that way. Women having the vote may be right, he said, "but we won't have it."

THE PROS AND CONS OF WOMEN'S SUFFRAGE

As women fought for the right to vote, both sides used advertisements and public postings to say why they were right and the other side was wrong. Below are summaries of some of the arguments. Some are funny, some not so much.

FOR WOMEN'S SUFFRAGE	AGAINST WOMEN'S SUFFRAGE
In states where women can vote, children are protected from working too much.	Voting is part of the feminist movement. To stop feminists, don't let women vote.
Women are as educated as men.	Most women don't want the ballot forced on them by the group of crazy women who do.
Women, why are you paid less than men, why do your children go to factories, why aren't you treated fairly in courts? Because you can't vote!	Remember that woman suffrage means suffrage for every woman and not only for your own female relatives, friends, and acquaintances.
If she's good enough to be a mother to a man's baby, she's good enough to vote with that man.	It will make women unladylike.

Often women who actively fought against the suffragists were wealthy or married to powerful men or both. These women enjoyed a social status that protected them from problems working women faced, like low pay and long working hours.

FIGHTING BACK: FLORENCE KELLEY

Some women argued that voting was necessary to lift up less fortunate women. Florence Kelley was born in 1859, and her parents encouraged her interest in social activism. "No one needs all the powers of the fullest citizenship more urgently than the wage-earning woman," she said in 1898. She fought for protections for all workers, including children who at that time had real jobs with long hours, and against racial discrimination.

PARADES AND PROTESTS

The time had come to use bolder tactics. Elizabeth Cady Stanton's daughter, Harriot Stanton Blatch, returned home to the United States in 1902 after living in Britain, and was among those who thought American women needed to embrace the tougher methods used by some of the women of Britain's suffrage movement.

British women were calling out politicians, holding huge and disruptive outdoor meetings, and organizing workers to join them in the fight.

BRITISH "SUFFRAGETTES"

The time period during which Americans were fighting for the right to vote overlapped with women in the United Kingdom doing the same. Women of the British movement are often called "suffragettes."

British journalists first used "suffragette" to make fun of the women and their cause; "-ette" is often attached to a word to describe something as small. Some British women decided to adopt the term for their own, even though it started as something mean. American women never took to it in the same way.

As tactics evolved, the suffrage movement lost one of its leaders. When Anthony died in 1906, her last act was to leave all her money to the suffrage cause. She expressed her intense frustration to NAWSA president Anna Howard Shaw shortly before her death: "To think I have had more than sixty years of hard struggle for a little liberty, and then to die without it seems so cruel."

Marches increased the visibility of the American suffrage movement. Women in Iowa and California marched in 1908; the first major suffrage parade occurred in New York City in 1910. As Harriot Stanton Blatch explained, "Men and women are moved by seeing marching groups of people and by hearing music far more than by listening to the most careful argument." Blatch felt that showing off their numbers and organizational talents would help convince people that women deserved the vote.

THE STORY OF THE SUFFRAGE DOLL

Even before the United States entered World War I in 1917, the fighting in other countries affected the U.S. economy, and those who sold cotton earned way less than they were used to because the price of cotton dropped. Americans were encouraged to be patriotic and "buy-a-bale" of cotton.

NAWSA president Shaw saw an opportunity. To gain favor in Southern states, she sent money to suffrage organizations in the South to buy cotton. And she had an idea of what they could make with the cotton. A Cincinnati artist drew a pattern for a suffragist doll—a rosy-cheeked, brown-haired girl wearing a long yellow dress, a yellow rose in her hair, and a tag on her front that said "Votes for Women." The pattern came with a small card that told people to "Buy-a-bale" and "Buy-a-doll" pattern and use all the cotton.

The doll is an example of the women understanding politics and finding a way both to help the country and to advertise the women's movement.

PRESIDENT WILSON AND WOMEN'S SUFFRAGE

Woodrow Wilson was to become president on March 4, 1913. Wilson had said negative things about the movement, and the women of the movement seized the moment.

They held a giant parade in Washington, D.C., on the day before he was to become president. A famous picture from that day, March 3, 1913, shows twenty-seven-year-old law school graduate Inez Milholland wearing a flowing white cape and a crown with a star, sitting on a white horse. She rode at the front of a parade of more than 5,000 women's suffrage supporters marching the route Wilson would take for his inauguration the next day. Many of the women wore all white to look unified as they marched, walking together toward the same goal.

"They wanted to take what had been more or less traditionally a very masculine streetscape, and they made it their own," said Janice Ruth, who helped put together a big suffrage exhibit at the Library of Congress in 2019.

Months of planning went into the 1913 event. Signs and banners read "Woman's Cause Is Man's—They Rise or Fall Together" and the simple slogan of "Votes for Women." The sign that led the parade was wordy but direct: "We Demand an Amendment to the Constitution of the United States Enfranchising the Women of This Country."

The parade was a huge success. But looking back, the racism and inattention to inclusivity displayed by the organizers must be noted. Organizers had to be reminded by national suffrage leaders to welcome women of color. On parade day, black women were asked to walk as a group in the back instead of with their own states; journalist Wells-Barnett refused. She marched alongside the white women of her home state of Illinois.

CONFRONTING, PICKETING, AND PERSUADING THE PRESIDENT

Even with more and more people learning about the movement and seeing the parades, suffrage remained an uphill climb during President Wilson's term. The proposed amendment had little to no support in Congress.

FIGHTING BACK: ANNA HOWARD SHAW

Suffrage leader Shaw didn't just have great ideas about dolls. She was also a minister and had a medical degree. In 1916, she faced off with President Wilson.

All the pressure and parades made Wilson come around, at least a little bit, to the idea of women voting. But he didn't want an amendment to the Constitution. Speaking at a women's suffrage convention in 1916, he said, "I have not come to ask you to be patient, because you have been," he said, adding that he knew they'd eventually win the right to vote. But, he said, "you can afford a little while to wait."

Shaw responded, "We have waited long enough for the vote, we want it now." She turned directly to Wilson with a smile. "And we want it to come during your administration."

The United States began to fight in World War I in 1917, and most suffragists pledged loyalty to the country. But unlike during the Civil War, they continued to demand the right to vote. Women protested at the White House daily, holding signs such as "Mr. President How Long Must

Women Wait for Liberty." When men assaulted some of the women, it was the women who were threatened with arrest. That year, more than 200 women were arrested.

Women flooded the White House with telegrams (the time period's version of an email) that complained of the arrests. In a July 18, 1917, message, suffragist leader Blatch wrote to President Wilson that he should give women the vote instead of jail sentences. The next day, a front-page article in the *New York Times* said Wilson was considering doing just that. The pressure had gotten to him.

October 1917 brought the final major suffrage parade, when women marched from Washington Square Park in the lower part of New York City in a three-hour procession that included farmers, factory workers, doctors, teachers, and social workers. The next month, New York women won the right to vote.

After New York passed its law, the U.S. House of Representatives again voted on the federal amendment, getting the exact number of votes needed to pass. But the Senate voted down the bill.

The leaders of the women's suffrage movement vowed to make the senators who voted no pay, and they did. They campaigned against their reelection and won enough seats to swing the Senate in the women's favor. On June 4, 1919, the Senate approved the amendment.

Congress had finally approved women's right to vote. Now, for the amendment to become official, thirty-six state governments needed to vote for it.

THE CONSTITUTIONAL AMENDMENT COMES DOWN TO TENNESSEE

After thirty-five states agreed to ratify, Tennessee was the last hope to win thirty-six states before the deadline of the 1920 presidential election. In August 1920, both activists in favor of the amendment and those fighting against it stayed at Nashville's Hermitage Hotel, close to the Tennessee state capitol. Suffragists passed out yellow roses and those against the amendment handed out red ones.

The vote was a nail-biter. A deciding vote would come from Harry Burn, a first-time legislator in his early twenties. The people Burn represented wanted him to vote no, and he wore a red anti-suffrage rose in his lapel as he prepared to vote. But in his pocket was a letter from his mother telling him to "be a good boy" and vote for women's suffrage. He listened to her and voted to approve women's right to vote.

A few days later, the Nineteenth Amendment was made official. August 26, 2020, marks the celebration of 100 years of women's suffrage.

WHAT WOMEN DID WITH THE VOTE

Two generations of women had to tune out countless nay-sayers, challenge authority at the highest level, and be willing to revamp their strategy over and over. They faced protesters at their parades and sometimes even time in jail. All for a right they should have had since the country's start.

The legendary journalist Cokie Roberts, who died in 2019, put it perfectly when she once interrupted her fellow reporter as he described the passage of the Nineteenth Amendment and its "granting women the right to vote."

"No, no, no, no! No granting!" Roberts said. "We had the right to vote as American citizens. We didn't have to be granted it by some bunch of guys."

Still, for many women of color, the Nineteenth Amendment would make little difference in their lives; they'd have to wait, sometimes all the way until the 1965 Voting Rights Act, to cast a ballot. Even as the Nineteenth Amendment was signed, minority women knew they still had to fight for their right to vote.

AFRICAN AMERICAN WOMEN TURNED AWAY FROM THE POLLS

Black women in Texas helped fight for women's right to vote, and the state government agreed to let women vote in 1918. When Election Day came, black women joined the white women they'd worked with, everyone dressed up for their first vote. But the African American women were told they couldn't vote; the only reason was the color of their skin. Christia Adair, an African American woman who was twenty-five years old at the time, remembered her sadness from that day when she told the story sixty years later. "That just hurt our hearts real bad," she said.

It took American women a little while to fully embrace their new right, and there wasn't the immediate rush to the polls one might expect. But women eventually grew into their power, and by 1980, the percentage of women who cast a ballot was higher than the percentage of men who did. And that's been true in every presidential election since.

After the 2018 elections, California congresswoman Nancy Pelosi, for the second time in her career, took the gavel as Speaker of the House, the most powerful position in the U.S. House of Representatives. For the first time, more than 100 women would serve in the 435-member U.S. House of Representatives.

Pelosi spoke to the members of the House on the day they took their oaths of office. "I'm particularly proud to be [a] woman Speaker of the House of this Congress, which marks the one hundredth year of women having the right to vote."

VOTING PROBLEMS AND VOTING SOLUTIONS

The right to vote is a necessary part of having personal freedom. A whopping 91 percent of us believe this, according to a 2017 Pew study.

But if we hold the right to vote so close to our hearts, then why don't all of us vote on Election Day?

TURNOUT STATISTICS

What do we mean by "not all of us vote"? Here's a break-down of how many Americans who were eligible to vote cast a ballot in recent elections:

- 2014:   42 percent
- 2016:   61 percent
- 2018:   53 percent

Why exactly are Americans so lazy about voting? First, I don't think we are. Many things can keep voters from the polls—work, lack of childcare, confusion over registration. Plus, some states don't always make it easy for everyone to vote. And even though the majority of us value voting as a right, the country doesn't always do a great job of explaining to younger generations the importance of voting and how it works. Voting is a right that's effective only when put into action.

To help improve voter turnout, we need to think about what keeps some people from voting, and ways that we can make it easier.

Doing that is actually something else Americans agree on. The same 2017 Pew study found nearly 60 percent of Americans believe "everything possible should be done to make it easy for every citizen to vote."

Jeremy Bird, who organized get-out-the-vote efforts for Barack Obama's successful 2012 presidential campaign, offers one big clue. Sometimes he begins speeches by asking how many people would have come to hear him talk if they'd had to sign up thirty days before. "If you had to get a stamp, put it in an envelope, and mail it? None of you would be here!" Bird's point raises the first hurdle people have to jump over before voting: having to register up to thirty days before an election in some states is one of the factors that keep people from voting.

REGISTERING TO VOTE

Once you reach the age of eighteen, you do have the right to vote. But you won't actually get to vote if you haven't *registered* in advance. It's kind of like RSVP'ing to a birthday party—you have to let your state know you're planning to be there.

States have very different rules for registration, so you'll need to check how your state does it. (North Dakota is the only state that doesn't require registration.)

How: Some states still require you to fill out a form, but most allow online registration.

When: How early you need to register also depends on your state—some states allow you to register on the same day you vote, others thirty days in advance. But if you're currently under eighteen, the first thing you should check is when you can register. Some states allow preregistration when you're sixteen or seventeen, so you can sign up in advance and be ready to go when the first election after you're eighteen rolls around.

What: You'll be asked for your name, date of birth, home address, and if you want to affiliate with a particular political party, like the Republicans or Democrats. Some states ask for a driver's license or ID number.

Automatic?: More and more states are using automatic voter registration (discussed in detail later), which means you might be automatically registered when you sign up for state-related services like a driver's license.

BONUS TIP:

You may be eligible to vote before you turn eighteen! In some states, you can vote in the primary election—when political parties choose their candidates for the general election— when you're seventeen as long as you'll be eighteen by Election Day.

WHAT ARE THE VOTING HOLDUPS?

There are voting rules that make it easier to vote and ones that make it difficult. Understanding some of the different rules helps us understand turnout. The most important thing to know may be this: each state sets many of its own rules about voting.

That means registration requirements, the state's voting period, and whether people can vote by mail, in person, or by absentee ballot, are different—sometimes very different—state to state. Historian and onetime British ambassador to the United States James Bryce said this: "I cannot attempt to describe the complicated and varying election laws of the different States."

It is clear what Bryce meant. My mom lives in suburban Houston. She cast her midterm election ballot during Texas's early voting period, more than a week before I voted on Election Day, the only day I could vote in New York. (After the 2018 election, New York finally approved early voting.) Some states require voters to show identification (IDs), but what counts as proper identification is state-specific; a bank statement works in West Virginia, for example, while a photo ID is needed in Mississippi. That modern-sounding Bryce quote? It's from 1888! We probably should have achieved more uniformity in 130 years.

One area states have historically handled very differently is voting by mail, also called vote-at-home. Washington, Oregon, Colorado, Hawaii, and Utah conduct their elections by mailing ballots to all eligible voters, and California is also increasingly using vote by mail. All states allow for vote by mail for absentee voting and in some elections at the discretion of state and local officials. While anyone can request an absentee ballot in many states, about a third require an "excuse," like the voter being out of town on Election Day.

Following the outbreak of the novel coronavirus in the

United States, voting experts and lawmakers called for states without readily available vote-by-mail programs to adopt them in order to avoid disruptions to the November 2020 election. It will be challenging for states not used to handling a lot of mail-in ballots, but experts believe it is possible if they make efforts to quickly begin their preparations. "Every state could do this," Kim Wyman, Washington's secretary of state, told the *Washington Post* in March of that year. But, she cautioned, "It takes time to ramp up."

DO RULES MAKE A DIFFERENCE IN TURNOUT? YES!

That lack of uniformity contributes to the differences in voter participation state to state. Let's compare two states that have among the best turnouts to two that often have the worst.

Maine and Minnesota: presidential turnout rate of about 70 percent.

Voters can register the same day as the election; they have long early voting periods and minimal voter ID requirements.

Texas and Tennessee: presidential turnout rate of 50 percent.

Voters must register thirty days before an election; they have shorter early voting periods.

Texans can't register online, and the state requires people seeking to register voters, such as in voter registration drives, to take a special class. Tennessee passed a similar law in 2019 that required training for larger voter registration drives and would fine groups that turn in incomplete forms. (Lawsuits are ongoing over the Tennessee law; a Tennessee

FELONS AND VOTING

The U.S. Constitution and laws require that citizens of all races, sexes, and religions must be able to vote. But there is a way states can prevent people from voting even if they're citizens over eighteen: if they've been convicted of a serious crime, called a felony. It's another area where states do things very differently, and it can mean that hundreds of thousands of people can't vote in certain states. An estimated six million American citizens cannot vote because of a prior felony conviction, a 2016 report said. If that group were a state, they'd be about the twentieth most populous.

The United States is one of only a few developed democracies where some felons don't regain their rights for years after they complete their sentences, and sometimes never do.

EXAMPLES OF HOW STATES TREAT FELONS AND VOTING

Vermont and Maine: People convicted of a felony can vote even when they're in prison.

Illinois, Ohio, Montana: People convicted of a felony can vote again as soon as they are released from prison.

Texas and Georgia: People convicted of a felony can vote only after they complete probation; that time period can be years.

Iowa: People convicted of a felony are barred for life from voting, unless they ask the government to make an exception specifically for them.

BONUS FACT

Many states' broad rules barring felons from voting arose after the Civil War. Laws that African Americans were considered more likely to break—or laws that were easy to convict African Americans for breaking, whether they'd done it or not—were specifically selected as ones that would result in giving up the right to vote. It was another way, often openly acknowledged, during and after Reconstruction to curb African Americans' right to vote. African Americans are still affected in a disproportionate way today.

This is an area of the law that's changing rapidly. Many states, either by vote or by actions by their governors, are restoring rights to convicted felons. Some states, however, are determined to keep their laws the same. That means whether or not a felon is eligible to vote depends on where they live.

VOTER SUPPRESSION AND FIGHTING AGAINST IT

Voter suppression is something that makes voting burdensome or really difficult. Examples of voter suppression include:

- moving voting locations too far from public transportation
- closing polling locations early in a way that prevents working people from voting
- not allowing students to use their college ID as their ID for voting
- being too aggressive in taking people off "voter rolls" (the list of people who can vote)
- delaying someone's registration if the name on their

voter registration doesn't exactly match what's on other state files. Not including the "Jr." in someone's name or including or removing a hyphen from a last name are examples of ways that can happen.

Mimi Marziani, president of the Texas Civil Rights Project, who teaches a law school class on election law, describes it this way: Voter suppression in the past was straightforward. In the days of Jim Crow laws, literacy tests and poll taxes were visible and obvious ways to keep minorities and poor people from voting. Even further back, it was simply illegal for those groups to vote. There was "a locked door right in front of you," and no key, she said.

Current voter suppression is a door that can be opened, but only by following a lot of very complicated steps. It doesn't mean voting is impossible, Marziani said, but it works because the harder you make it to vote, the greater a voter's desire has to be to take all the steps. And if that desire hasn't been planted by parents or educators or friends, or one has a job with specific hours, or any of the many other reasons that might stop someone from voting are present, those temporary blocks can be effective.

THE VOTING RIGHTS ACT NOW

When voting laws appear to unfairly impact minority

groups, the people affected can sue the state or city or county under the Voting Rights Act (VRA), first passed in 1965.

FAMOUS EXAMPLES OF VRA SUCCESSES

- In 1972, Andrew Young became the first African American elected to the U.S. House of Representatives in Georgia in one hundred years. He ran a good campaign and knocked on his neighbors' doors, but he also had to use the VRA to challenge polling location changes in his district because they affected African American voters much more than white voters.

- In the early 1980s, skeptical lawmakers did not want to renew parts of the VRA, but they did after hearing testimony from a fifty-year-old teacher and activist in Alabama who described how officials intimidated African American voters—including not letting them vote in private—and that voting was open only during work hours when many could not make it.

For many years, states that had a history of unfair voting laws were required to get approval from the federal government before they enacted new voting laws. The laws could be reviewed to see if they were going to be harmful to voters of a particular race.

But in 2013, in a decision referred to as *Shelby County*, the U.S. Supreme Court struck down part of the law that determined which states should be monitored, and the result was that no more monitoring would happen unless Congress reworked the law. The chief justice of the United States, John Roberts, thought the part of the law that required some states to get approval for new voting laws was outdated.

The *Shelby* decision wasn't a court decision where you had to wait long to see the impact. Right away, Texas and North Carolina put into effect laws that voting activists said would be harmful to minority groups. Texas enacted a voter ID law, and North Carolina enforced several new voting laws, including a limit on early voting and a limit on the ways people could register to vote.

Courts eventually struck down the laws (Texas passed a different voter ID law later that is now in effect), but it showed how fighting the laws would now have to work: instead of states checking with the federal government first, groups may have to sue and take the issue all the way through the court process. It often takes a lot of time, and citizens can be affected in the meantime.

FIGHTING VOTER SUPPRESSION

Voter suppression is something most people only think about at election time, but there are people who always keep an eye on it. "Voter suppression is tricky because the pieces that are put in place to lead to voter suppression happen in between elections," said Celina Stewart, senior director of advocacy and litigation for the League of Women Voters.

THE LEAGUE OF WOMEN VOTERS

The League of Women Voters was founded by suffrage leader Carrie Chapman Catt in 1920, about six months before the Nineteenth Amendment gave women the right to vote nationwide. The League's earliest mission was to encourage and prepare women to use their new power at the ballot box.

In the one hundred years since, the League has fought for laws to promote greater access to the polls, including expansions of the Voting Rights Act and the federal law that says citizens must be able to register to vote at state driver's license offices. With more than 750 League chapters located throughout the nation, they are a go-to source for voter registration drives and concerns about any unfair voting practices. The bottom line: if you have a question about voting, your local chapter of the League of Women Voters can probably answer it.

Another organization very active in the fight against voter suppression is the American Civil Liberties Union. The ACLU's purpose is to defend and preserve the rights (the "civil liberties") guaranteed by the Constitution, including voting, which they describe as "the cornerstone of our democracy and the fundamental right upon which all our civil liberties rest." The ACLU has offices in every state.

Dale Ho is a lawyer in charge of the ACLU's voting rights division. He was part of the team that fought the North Carolina changes, and oversees lawsuits throughout the country.

Ho pins the efforts to suppress the vote as revving up a few years into the Obama administration, even before *Shelby County*. By October 2012, nineteen states had passed laws or begun policies that could make it more difficult to vote. Some of these laws were overturned by courts, some were pushed back by voters, and some were upheld by courts. But the number of them shows that adding new barriers to voting was important to some state legislators.

FIGHTING BACK: DALE HO

Ho was inspired when he studied the civil rights movement in school, especially by lawyers' work that helped make sure African American children could go to the same schools as white children.

Some people are great at talking to groups and motivating people and leading movements, but Ho said he prefers to read and write, and thought that being a lawyer would be his best way to contribute. He works on cases that the ACLU believes will make voting opportunities equal for every American.

Even though Ho might prefer to work quietly in his office, sometimes he has to do some pretty serious public speaking: in 2019, he argued in front of the U.S. Supreme Court over whether a question about people's citizenship should appear on the official U.S. count of who lives in the country, called the Census. Ho said that such a question was harmful. His side won.

MONITORING WHO IS ON THE VOTER LISTS

One issue being watched closely is the "purging" of voter rolls. Purging means removing people from the list of people who can vote. If a person is purged from the role, that person needs to register again or otherwise clear up their status to be able to vote. States and municipalities want to have clean voter rolls. People need to be removed from the rolls if they die or move, and laws require states to try to stay up to date.

Some states have gotten aggressive about culling their rolls, and the methods can have a disproportionate impact on minority voters. A study showed counties and states that previously required approval for changes in voting laws were found to be the ones doing most of the purging.

States are more emboldened to cull their lists following a 2018 Supreme Court decision called *Husted v. A. Philip Randolph*. The *New York Times* described the court's decision: states can "kick people off the rolls if they skip a few elections and fail to respond to a notice from election officials."

Not all states are this aggressive, but it's a good reminder to stay on top of your registration status, once you're old enough to register.

VOTING TIP:

The best way to avoid being incorrectly taken off the rolls is to keep your information up to date and not skip elections. It's also always best to confirm your registration before each election, prior to when your state's registration period ends.

WHAT IS VOTER FRAUD?

Voter ID laws, the purging of voter rolls, and limits on making registration more accessible are often done in the name of preventing voter fraud. Someone pretending they are someone else when they vote, or someone casting a ballot when they know they aren't allowed to, is obviously wrong and a misuse of the voting system. It's also extremely risky; punishment can be thousands of dollars of fines and even jail time, as well as deportation for non-citizens.

But voter fraud of that sort rarely happens. The cases of people getting in legal trouble for voter fraud are few, and often the person who has attempted to vote when they shouldn't made a mistake, such as thinking they could vote because they have legal documentation saying they can live in the country. Even considering the few cases where people who shouldn't vote make it through the checks and cast a ballot, the total number represents less than a drop of water in the ocean of ballots cast.

In a lawsuit over a Kansas voter registration requirement designed to prevent voter fraud, it was revealed that over a twenty-year-period, fewer than forty noncitizens attempted to register in one Kansas county that had 130,000 voters. Most of those forty were mistakes rather than intentional fraud, and only five actually cast a ballot.

THE PRESENT AND FUTURE
OF VOTING

Understanding that voter suppression does happen is important, said Jeanette Senecal, senior director of impact for the League of Women Voters. But she worries that too much focus on suppression might actually suppress the vote even more.

Her message to potential voters: if you confirm you're properly registered, know available voting methods and locations, and give yourself time to get to the polls and wait in line if necessary, you can vote.

MAKING SURE YOU CAN VOTE

Before Election Day, follow the registration and voting

procedures for your state. There are plenty of websites to help you. Each state has a secretary of state website that includes voting regulations and important dates, but free private services will go the extra mile and text or email you as deadlines approach.

TOP QUESTIONS OF VOTERS

The League of Women Voters has an information site, VOTE411.org, where people can find all the information they need about registration and voting in their state. Senecal said they make sure to have the answers to the top three questions voters ask:

- Am I registered?

- Where's my polling place?

- What's on my ballot?

VOTING TIP:

We don't always know what we need, so make it easier and let the experts help you. When it's time, sign up for those alerts!

AUTOMATIC VOTER REGISTRATION

Voting advocates point to two things that can make registering to vote easier: automatic voter registration (AVR) and same day registration (SDR).

Automatic voter registration means that when an eligible state citizen interacts with a government agency—like the Department of Motor Vehicles—the information needed to register to vote is transferred electronically to election officials. Though there are some checks to make sure everything is in order, the person is then registered. Why is this helpful to would-be voters? They don't have to fill out an extra form.

Also, if a voter updates their personal information with a government office, such as when they move, their voting info is also updated. In states that don't have AVR, a person usually has to update in two places—their driver's license and their voter information.

AVR is a relatively new option. In 2016, Oregon was the first state to give it a try. Since then, more than a dozen states have adopted it, either by citizens voting for it or legislatures passing laws in favor of it. The benefits of AVR go beyond convenience for the voters; there's plenty in it for the states as well.

"It's a cost savings. It's efficiency. It results in more accurate [voter] rolls," said Paul Gronke, a political science professor at Reed College in Portland and an expert on electoral behavior and voting laws.

The 2016 presidential election was the first after Oregon instituted AVR, and its benefits were notable.

Gronke and his colleagues found that nearly 100,000 eligible citizens newly registered through AVR voted in the 2016 presidential election. Though turnout can't all be attributed to AVR, it certainly didn't hurt: 70 percent of Oregon's voting-age population voted, a state record.

Those who registered via AVR were more likely to live outside cities, in low-income areas, low-education areas, and racially diverse areas, the Oregon study found. So at least in Oregon, AVR reached voters who were likely to have political opinions that represent both Democrats and Republicans.

Like anything else in the voting world, AVR is not without its critics. They are concerned that failures by government agencies or outdated state technology could result in noncitizens being registered. California was criticized during early implementation of its AVR program. Its Department of Motor Vehicles admitted in 2018 it may have registered 1,500 noncitizens and improperly classified the preferred political party and vote-by-mail preferences of about 23,000 citizens. (The DMV said the mistake was theirs; the noncitizens had not sought to be registered and did not actually vote.) In April 2019, a *Los Angeles Times* editorial said that while the kickoff of the program was "a disaster," AVR was fulfilling its promise a year in—with one million new voters registered.

The issues of outdated systems are something states (and state budgets) must address, but the fact is that where AVR is instituted, it works. In 2019, the Brennan Center released a study showing voter registration rates greatly improved everywhere AVR was used. Brennan Center official Myrna Pérez said at the time: "We should be making it as easy as possible for eligible citizens to vote, and that begins with getting registered. Our current voter registration systems are [outdated]. We're at a moment of great reform, and our election systems are overdue for an upgrade. As states continue to enact restrictive voting laws, AVR is a needed change."

Registration, of course, doesn't guarantee voting. In some states that use AVR, voters who sought out registration, rather than being registered through AVR, were more likely to actually vote. It means efforts must be made to get new registrants to vote—but a person certainly can't vote if they're not registered.

SAME DAY REGISTRATION

Another change to consider? Allowing same day registration, where citizens can register and vote on the same day.

More than a quarter of states already have same day registration. Maine, Minnesota, and Wisconsin have been doing it since the 1970s, and more states are considering it. Maryland and Michigan voters elected to add themselves to the list in 2018, and California announced in 2019 it would allow voters to register same day at local polling stations.

FUN FACTS: MINNESOTA

Minnesota's nickname is the North Star state, and it's definitely a star when it comes to voting. In addition to having same day registration since the 1970s and regularly leading the nation in turnout, it holds the all-time state turnout record—79 percent in 2004. When George W. Bush won reelection for president that year, 20 percent of people who voted in Minnesota registered the same day.

"It's easy for voters to understand [having] to register and to vote the same day," the League's Stewart said. "Those are the things that we have to think about when we're thinking about remedies to voter suppression."

Using AVR nationwide could directly impact the way campaigns are run, according to Jeremy Bird, the former Obama staffer: "We spend tens of millions of dollars, probably hundreds of millions, registering voters. We could spend that money educating people and getting them out to vote."

A DIFFERENT WAY TO VOTE:
RANKED-CHOICE VOTING

If someone asked me my favorite candy, I'd probably say gummy worms. But I also love Nerds and sour jelly beans. I do NOT like licorice.

This happens sometimes with candidates, too. Voters may have a candidate they like the most, some maybe a little less, and some they don't like at all. Usually voters can choose only one and have no way to show their preferences for the others.

Ranked-choice voting gives them the possibility of their vote counting for their second choice if their first choice doesn't win.

Let's say there are four candidates: Aubrie, Bryan, Carson, Debbie.

Voters mark which one is their first choice, second choice, and so on. When the votes are counted, if one of the four receives a majority (more than 50 percent) of the votes, they win.

I want Debbie to win, so I mark her as my first choice. Carson is my second favorite, Bryan third, and Aubrie fourth.

When the votes are all counted, if no candidate gets more than 50 percent of the vote, the fourth-place finisher is eliminated.

In this race, my first choice of Debbie came in last. She is out! But I and all the people who voted for Debbie will still have our votes counted in the next round. Carson, my second-place choice, gets my vote in the second round.

Those votes are counted for the appropriate candidate, and if that count is enough to give Aubrie, Bryan, or Carson a majority, they'll win. If not, the counting continues.

Ranked-choice voting isn't just theoretical. Cambridge, Massachusetts, for example, has used it for more than seventy years. In June 2018, Maine became the first state to use it in a statewide election. Other U.S. cities use it too, and in 2019, New York City voters voted to have it in future local elections.

PART TWO

KNOW BEFORE YOU VOTE

WHAT IS GERRYMANDERING?

Now that everyone who's eligible is on their way to vote—or so we hope—and you know when the first time you'll be able to vote is, it's time to dive a little deeper into related, often controversial, topics that affect voting.

Take gerrymandering. *Gerrymander* is a funny word. It's a combination of the last name of Elbridge Gerry, who was governor of Massachusetts in 1812, and *salamander*, a lizard-like creature.

Understanding what gerrymandering is requires some background.

BACKGROUND INFO

- Members of the U.S. House of Representatives each represent a specific district in their home state.

- There are 435 total districts.

- If you live in a small town, your district probably includes your town and those nearby. If you live in a big city, that city might be split into a few districts, or share a district with a smaller town nearby.

- How many districts each state has depends on its population—how many people live in the state.

- A state's official population is determined every ten years (in the zero years, like 2000, 2010, and 2020) by the U.S. Census.

- After the official count, the 435 seats of the U.S. House of Representatives are divided among the states, in proportion to their population. After the 2010 Census count, California had the largest population and the most U.S. House seats, with fifty-three. Florida had twenty-seven, and states with the smallest populations, like Wyoming, have only one.

- States have to draw district boundary lines to divide up their states into the number of districts they have, and each district is required to have about the same number of people.

- Who draws those lines and how is when gerrymandering can come into play.

What does the mash-up word that is gerrymandering have to do with districts?

Sometimes districts are drawn specifically to include people who the politicians drawing the lines think will vote a certain way. That often means the political party of the person who will win the district is predictable even before the election happens. That's gerrymandering.

Think of it this way: Say you were voting on what color is the best, and you wanted blue to win. If you have seven friends, and you know three of them like blue, and four like other colors, you would make sure to include the three "blue" friends in your district and put the ones who didn't like blue in another district. That way when you took a vote on the best color, you'd already know what color is going to win your district.

HOW DO THEY KNOW HOW PEOPLE WILL VOTE?

Knowing how people will vote is actually the easy part. In many states, people designate which party they identify with when they register to vote, so sometimes whether you identify as a Republican or a Democrat is public information. Further, mapmakers can predict voter behavior in a geographic area by looking at public information about voters in the area, like the breakdown of votes in previous elections and data from Census responses. The biggest indicator is a geographic one: people who live in cities are more likely to vote Democrat, while Republican voters dominate rural areas. Sophisticated mapping programs compile all the data and offer up thousands of options for mapmakers to choose from.

GERRYMANDERING NOW

Gerrymandering has gone on for a very long time, and both parties have done it when they have the chance. But in the past few years it's become more of an issue.

"Gerrymandering has exploded in the public [awareness] in the last two years . . . because there was a clear pattern of Republican advantage versus their share of the vote," said David Wasserman, an editor of the nonpartisan Cook Political Report and an expert in U.S. House of Representatives politics.

What Wasserman means is that because of the way U.S. district lines were drawn in certain states, Republicans had many more U.S. House of Representative seats than one would expect if they saw the total state votes.

AN EARLY LOVE OF MAPS

Wasserman knows a lot about U.S. congressional districts. He knows about their representatives, their demographic makeup, their voting histories. When it comes to district boundaries, he's very good at predicting how changes would impact the House of Representatives.

He's been interested in maps for a very long time. Wasserman never forgot one of his elementary school teachers, who encouraged what he called his "weird" interest in drawing maps. The teacher even saved for more than twenty-five years a map of Wasserman's neighborhood he drew as a kid. Wasserman's advice: don't forget to tell your favorite teachers how much you appreciate them.

An example of recent gerrymandering: For the last several U.S. House elections in North Carolina, the Democrats have won close to half the votes statewide (so if you count up all the votes in the state, about half the people voted for a Democrat). But Democrats won only three out of thirteen congressional seats. The lines were drawn to group Democratic and Republican voters in such a way that even with their strong presence in the state, Democrats weren't the majority in most of the congressional districts.

POLITICAL JARGON: PACKING AND CRACKING

In gerrymandering terms:

Packing: taking a lot of people who are likely to vote for the same party and stuffing as many of them as you can fit into one district.

Cracking: spreading people who are likely the same party into several different districts.

WHY PACK OR CRACK?

- In a packed district, that party will win the district by a lot. It's a way to "waste" a lot of votes if it isn't the line drawer's preferred party. It means the party not preferred by the line drawer will win a district, but it'll win fewer districts than if the people were spread across multiple districts.

- Cracking people into a lot of different districts mean the people "cracked" won't have large enough numbers in those districts to win.

WHO DRAWS THE LINES?

Gerrymandering doesn't happen in every state. It usually happens in states where district lines are drawn by state lawmakers. (Not all states have lawmakers draw the lines.) And even in the states where the lawmakers draw the lines, maps that favor one party are usually only possible if that party is the majority in the state legislature and there is a governor of the same party, too. (The governor part isn't necessary if the governor doesn't have the right to "veto"—or refuse to sign—a new map.)

States where gerrymandering has been a big issue—and the subject of many lawsuits—in recent years include Ohio, Maryland, North Carolina, Pennsylvania, Texas, and Wisconsin. In states like these, the map of congressional districts often looks kind of strange—they might have lines that zigzag up and down and right to left all over the state. Some recent nicknames people have given to the way these districts look—like the way the 1812 Massachusetts area was said to look like a salamander—include:

- Wile E. Coyote on a Hoverboard Behind Peppa Pig (North Carolina)
- Fajita Strip (Texas)
- Broken-Winged Pterodactyl (Maryland)

IS GERRYMANDERING LEGAL?

You may be wondering if gerrymandering is okay for law-makers to do. Are there any limits on it?

In 1986, the U.S. Supreme Court said districts cannot be drawn in a way that discriminates against a minority group by preventing them from electing a candidate of their own choice. That is called racial gerrymandering. That means an area of predominantly black residents shouldn't be split in three ways and grouped with majority white districts. Forbidding this kind of racial gerrymandering has resulted in the election of more representatives from minority groups.

The type of gerrymandering that has been a big issue lately is partisan gerrymandering—drawing lines to benefit one political party over the other. In 2019, partisan gerrymandering was a focus in two very different high-profile places: first, the U.S. Supreme Court. And second, a documentary movie in New York City featuring Katie Fahey, a young woman who took on partisan gerrymandering in her home state.

A TRIP TO THE U.S. SUPREME COURT

The U.S. Supreme Court has nine justices, and for several months every year they hear arguments on the most important legal cases in the country. The arguments happen in one large courtroom in Washington, D.C., in a building not far from the U.S. Capitol. The justices' job is to interpret the Constitution and laws of the United States, and their decisions are the final word on the law. We've talked about many Supreme Court decisions in this book, but before the decision comes, the people and organizations involved in the lawsuits—and those who are going to be affected by them—have a chance to explain their positions and arguments to the justices.

In March 2019, the U.S. Supreme Court justices listened to arguments in two partisan gerrymandering cases. One was over North Carolina's district lines—the ones where there were ten Republicans and three Democrats. The other was over lines in Maryland, where Democrats in power had drawn lines that took away the one district in Maryland that usually went Republican.

The question the Supreme Court justices had to answer: Is it okay for lawmakers to draw district lines that favor their own party, especially when it doesn't match with the political makeup of voters in their state?

It was early spring in Washington, D.C., and the cherry blossoms bloomed pink. A long line of tourists hoping to see the arguments wrapped around the building, but the grand plaza in front of the famous Supreme Court steps was empty as I walked to the side entrance designated for press.

Reporters can't bring in phones or computers, and no pictures are allowed. There are also no video cameras in the courtroom, so if you want to listen to the arguments later, a voice recording is the only option. An artist sits in court and draws pictures of the justices arguing the cases.

We scrambled to our feet when the justices entered the room, as is tradition, and the justices took their seats in their tall-back leather chairs. The chief justice, John Roberts, sits in the middle.

The League of Women Voters was one of the groups arguing against gerrymandering in the North Carolina case. Those participating in a lawsuit write long papers to the court, called "briefs," that tell the justices what their legal arguments are. In its briefs, the League of Women Voters told the court that the North Carolina maps "cracked and packed" Democratic voters throughout the state, so that those voters' votes carried less weight than they would in a fairly drawn district.

Lawyers for the state of North Carolina argued that their district lines were fine. They said "the framers assigned the . . . political task of districting to political actors"—politicians in state legislatures—and oversight of the fairness to Congress. The founders of the country knew, in other words, that political parties would draw lines in their own favor, and they were okay with it.

North Carolina's lawyers also argued it's too difficult for the court to design a test for how much partisanship—politicians trying to get their own party members in office—is too much.

The court doesn't make their decision the same day as the arguments; they take a few months to think about it and write a formal opinion.

Three months after the argument, a majority of the court, in a five-to-four vote, said there wasn't anything they could do about partisan gerrymandering. "Excessive partisanship in districting leads to results that reasonably seem unjust," Chief Justice Roberts wrote. Roberts understands, in other words, that it may seem unfair. But, he continued, it was a question about politics that was outside the powers of the U.S. courts.

Justice Elena Kagan wrote that she disagreed with the decision (officially called a dissent) with "deep sadness."

The Supreme Court decision shuts the door to protesting partisan maps in federal court, but lawsuits in state court over state laws and maps can continue. And where it's allowed by state law, citizens can still try to get their state courts to outlaw partisan gerrymandering in their state, or even vote on requiring a new way of drawing the maps.

The exact rules and plans are different from state to state. But the idea is to have a group of citizens made up of people from both parties (and sometimes people who aren't a member of either party) draw or approve the lines, or to still let legislatures do it, but not allow them to consider political parties when drawing the lines.

VOTING LINGO: BALLOT INITIATIVE

Ballot initiative—a question over a law or policy that is put on the ballot for citizens to vote for or against on Election Day.

- They can cover all sorts of topics. Whether convicted felons should be allowed to vote in Florida was a ballot initiative, and a North Dakota one asked whether volunteer firefighters should have special license plates.

- In the case of gerrymandering, the ballot initiative question might be whether to outlaw partisan gerrymandering, or whether to change how district lines are drawn.

A TWENTY-SEVEN-YEAR-OLD SLAYS THE GERRYMANDER DRAGON

Michigan is one of the states that, in certain circumstances, allows citizens to propose a state constitutional amendment by a ballot initiative.

Katie Fahey was twenty-seven years old and working for the Michigan Recycling Coalition during the 2016 election. Afterward, she felt sad about how ugly the election felt. Fahey believed gerrymandering was partly to blame for some of the angry political feelings in her state.

She took her frustration to Facebook. She wanted to take on gerrymandering in Michigan, she wrote. Did anyone want to help? She added the smiley-face emoji and posted. It turned out many people did.

WHEN DID KATIE FAHEY LEARN ABOUT GERRYMANDERING?

She learned in elementary school the definition of gerrymandering and how it worked, and remembers feeling like it was an unfair way to do things. She raised her hand and asked why no one was doing anything about it. "It really bothered me," she said. When students in Michigan learn about gerrymandering, they're now likely to learn about her fight against it.

Fahey found out that in Michigan they could try to stop gerrymandering by proposing a ballot initiative where voters could approve a change to the state constitution to create a commission with a mix of Republicans,

Democrats, and people who weren't members of either party to draw Michigan's district maps.

The law said she needed signatures from 315,000 Michigan citizens to get the question on the ballot. So she and her army of volunteers held thirty-three meetings in thirty-three days to gather signatures, educate people about the issue, and hear what citizens wanted in the amendment.

FAHEY'S VOLUNTEERS

- "Voters Not Politicians" is the name of their group.

- "Slay the Dragon" is their motto, and they wore T-shirts with a picture of the original gerrymander "salamander."

- Places they visited to get signatures included carnivals, highway rest stops, and churches.

DID THEY GET ENOUGH SIGNATURES?

- Yes! They got about 425,000 Michigan citizens to sign saying they wanted the ballot initiative on their 2018 ballot.

Fahey used Facebook Video to update her followers along the way, whether with total excitement after getting more signatures or in tears when it seemed like all their hard work might be tossed aside.

Election Night 2018 arrived after months of Fahey and her fellow volunteers traveling across the state to talk to voters. She walked around a ballroom nervously until she was told the citizens of Michigan had voted in favor of the ballot initiative. It won by about a million votes! The voters did want to have a commission draw their district lines.

"It felt amazing," she said. "So many people had said that regular people are never going to care about this issue and it's not going to pass."

Because it's politics, the battle in Michigan isn't over. Lawsuits continue over whether the commission should be put in place. Voters Not Politicians is fighting those claims and working to have it up and running by 2022.

Fahey's fight was part of a gerrymandering documentary, *Slay the Dragon*, which premiered in New York City at the Tribeca Film Festival in the spring of 2019. Fahey posed on the red carpet wearing her uniform of a neat blazer and a Slay the Dragon T-shirt. The movie is "a rallying cry about voting equality, and it really ends with this message of 'you can make the change,'" said Neal Block, one of the movie executives who decided to put it in theaters.

THE NEWS: YOUR SUPERPOWER

When it comes to voting, a top concern for young people is feeling like they don't know enough about the candidates or issues.

And that's totally understandable—we live in a world where social media, television, podcasts, and websites bombard us with constant information. But knowing which of it to read, or even which of it to believe, can be difficult. Understanding the news today, says actress and activist Yara Shahidi, requires figuring out so much political jargon that it can keep people from voting.

The remedy: a steady diet of news that gives it to you straight is a voter's superpower. Being an educated voter is something worth taking seriously.

While completely ridding the news of political jargon is unlikely, this section on becoming an educated voter aims to help you learn:

- that news sources that give you the political news you need to be an informed citizen are abundant and easy to find; and
- that the best way to avoid being tricked by something that isn't real is to know exactly where your information is coming from, and what purpose it's trying to serve.

CLASSIFYING INFORMATION

The first step in becoming an informed voter is learning to identify the types of information that are likely coming at you from social media and everywhere else.

"We have more incredible information literally available at our fingertips than ever before, but it's competing with so much more information intended to sell, persuade, mislead, incite, and misinform," said Alan Miller, award-winning journalist and founder of the News Literacy Project, a nonprofit organization that helps educators give students the tools to become informed and civically minded news consumers.

CNN's chief media correspondent, Brian Stelter, put the challenges we face in a more colorful way: "We're all walking into this overwhelming, intoxicating [game room], every day. . . . It's open at all hours. There are all these flashing lights, all of these stimuli that are encouraging us to stay."

Through both in-person seminars and online lessons for

educators moderated by active journalists, the News Literacy Project seeks to enable students to think like journalists and feel empowered in understanding and sharing information, Miller said. It's especially important in an environment where nearly everyone shares news and information via social media.

Part of the process is classifying the kind of information you take in. Here's a brief description of the types of information the News Literacy Project helps students learn about.

NEWS

- Verified, fact-based information presented in a neutral manner, as unbiased as possible.

- Should be the most relevant and timely information available.

- Should provide multiple perspectives.

- Should make you feel informed but free to make up your own mind.

RAW INFORMATION

- Information not processed through any news or opinion filter, like live video, a 911 call, or a court document.

- Remember it might not be the full story. What's out of frame or on the pages not shown? What happened before or after? How do we know the person talking is telling the truth?

- Journalists should help contextualize the information; wait to form an opinion until you have some of the context.

OPINION

- Designed to convince you of something, like which candidate to vote for or which policy to favor.

- The source of opinions is important—is it someone who knows what they're talking about?

- Is the information supported by facts? (It should be, especially in the news context.)

- The best opinion pieces address the points, good and bad, of the other side.

ADVERTISEMENT

- Paid for by a company or organization to try to sell you something, whether it's toothpaste or a political candidate.

- It wants you to feel like you really need what they're telling you about or, for politicians, like your life will be better if you vote for them.

ENTERTAINMENT

- Designed to be enjoyed—to make you laugh, cry, or to feel like an escape from your day.

- Entertainment can definitely include newsy information—comedy shows talk about the news all the time, for instance. Consider, though, whether something is entertainment first, education second.

PROPAGANDA

- False or misleading information created to misinform its audience.

- Usually this type of information doesn't want you just to think it's true; it also wants to make you upset, angry, frightened, or to blame someone.

- The language is aggressive, like "Can you believe they . . ." Or "They're trying to take from you . . ."

- The deliverer of the news may shout or use graphic images.

NEWS TIP:

My quick take on when to totally discard what someone's saying: if they're yelling at you and telling only one side of the story, or portraying someone as a hero with no faults, they're doing you no service. If you see a "news" organization doing that—change the channel, close the browser, or log off social media.

The primary information you want to use to help you become an informed citizen and voter is news—information someone has checked to make sure it's true and presented to you in a way that tells you the full story but doesn't try to form your opinion for you. It's information not just about the candidate, but about events and issues candidates will have to make decisions about. Other than propaganda, which can be extremely harmful, the other types of information have their places and can serve an important purpose. But the news is the most important thing to understand and follow.

THE ROLE OF A FREE PRESS

The founders of this country thought the role of the press was vital enough to mention it early in the Bill of Rights (the first ten amendments to the Constitution). That doesn't mean the founders didn't sometimes complain about news stories. They definitely did. But they also knew just how important a free press is to democracy.

The First Amendment says that Congress cannot pass laws "abridging" the press. Over time, courts have said that means the government must let the press do its job. It can't jail a reporter for publishing a story that criticizes the government, or shut down a newspaper because a politician doesn't like what it wrote.

WHAT DO I MEAN BY *PRESS*?

There are many ways to define *press*, but in this case, I mean news organizations—whether it's a news website, a newspaper, a television news channel like ABC or CNN, magazines, or podcasts—whose goal is to be honest and gather information to keep the public informed about events, information, and people that impact the world.

The press works for the public in a similar way that government officials do. Its job is to inform you of things going on in your community, your city, your country, and the world. Political stories also provide the details people want to know about candidates. And the most important part of doing all that is to tell you the truth, to act as a check on those in office and those seeking office, and to give you the information you need to make an informed decision.

If a candidate is taking bribes or city officials are hiding knowledge that toxic chemicals are in the drinking water, the press should help hold them accountable by telling the public.

News organizations are not perfect. Reporters sometimes make mistakes on facts, what should and shouldn't be the subject of a story, and even how the story is told. But the fact that mistakes happen is not a reason to mistrust all news coverage. Know that a good news organization always corrects its mistakes, quickly and prominently. (And should be called on it when they don't.)

THE PARTS OF A NEWS STORY

News stories—not opinion pieces, but straight-up news stories—answer the who, what, where, when, and why questions. Again, they serve to inform, not to convince. They might be breaking news (who won the New Hampshire primary or a governor resigning under a cloud of scandal), feature stories (details about jobs a candidate had before running for public office), or investigative pieces that have taken months to research and report. But they try to present facts, explain the different sides of an argument, and put the information into the context of areas it might affect.

There's no way I can run down all the sources that are credible and all that aren't, but I can talk about characteristics of trustworthy content and how a reputable news organization builds a story.

Think about it like you would when you're finding information for reports for school. You can't just include anything someone says on Wikipedia. You have to be sure the information comes from a reliable source who has done the right homework. It's the same with news sources. Consider what you need them to provide you, and the standards you need them to meet.

THE HALLMARKS OF A PROPER NEWS STORY

When reading a news story, the first question you need to ask is, where is this person getting the information? Did they see it or hear it themselves? Were they at the press conference or congressional hearing or did they talk to the people who did attend? Did they interview the people quoted themselves?

NEWS TIP

If you're reading news online or from social media and the story is a rehash of an article that links to the original, always check out the original source, too.

Michael Schmidt has been a *New York Times* reporter for more than a decade and covers national security and federal investigations. Schmidt was part of reporting teams that won two Pulitzers, the journalism world's top prize.

Schmidt took an hour's break from reporting to discuss with me how he builds stories. We settled into the bland bustle of a café near the *Times*'s Washington bureau for our interview. Like all reporters working today, he knows people distrust the media, though even that involves figuring out what "media" means. Newspapers? Partisans on cable news shows? Anyone with a Twitter account? "We all get lumped together," he said, "and we all don't have the same standards, biases, or beliefs."

There is no official list of rules all media follow, but there are codes of ethics and basic rules that guide any reputable journalist. The simplest is: don't put information out there unless you're as positive as you can possibly be that it's true. Check your facts. But also make sure you've:

- tried to get a comment from the involved parties
- included all relevant information
- made clear what you know and what you don't.

"We [need] to do more explaining of what we actually do," Schmidt said, to help the public understand "that we're nonpartisan fact-finders that go out and try and take a snapshot of the world every day and tell you what's going on. It's an imperfect medium. It's a very difficult thing to make a judgment about something on a day-to-day basis. But it is not a partisan exercise. It's an exercise in trying to dig as far and hard into the facts as possible."

So how does a reporter do this? A comic book describes Clark Kent sitting at his desk at the *Daily Planet* newspaper waiting for scoops. No disrespect to Superman, but that is definitely not how it works.

Political reporters covering a candidate or a race work to get to know not just the candidate, but the campaign staff, volunteers, people the candidate used to work with, election officials, opponent's staff, subject matter experts who can provide insight on policy, and on and on.

Building a network of sources and learning about your subject is the only way a reporter can be successful at informing the public, Schmidt said. "We have to use the tools that we have . . . to go out and see things, to listen to things, and to build relationships with people who will provide us with a greater understanding of something."

The bottom line is this: when reading or watching or listening to political news, the stories you can trust the most are the ones written or told by the person who gathered the information—they witnessed the event or talked to people who did, talked to people who disagreed, and can give you context as to why it mattered or didn't. You want your news to come as straight from the reporter to you as possible.

SPOTTING AN UNFAIR STORY, AND WHAT HAPPENS WHEN A REPORTER GETS IT WRONG

Before a story is published, reputable news organizations give people who are the story's focus or are mentioned in a way they might take issue with a chance to respond. "No surprises!" is something editors say all the time. No one should read the news and be shocked at what they see about themselves.

That means reporters often have the tough task of telling someone a story is going to run that is critical of the way they do their job. If you're reading a story that seems particularly harsh, always look to see how the person criticized responded. If you don't see quotes from that person or company, a sentence that they declined to comment or couldn't be reached, or information on that person's position, it could be a sign that the reporter didn't do their job and the news organization isn't one that should be trusted as a primary news source.

Despite all the checks in place, mistakes happen. It can be as simple as a misspelled name or an incorrect title, or something substantive like incorrectly describing a politician's position on a controversial issue. "Reporters live in fear of making mistakes," said CNN's Stelter. "There's nothing more embarrassing."

Schmidt echoed to me just how awful it feels to get something wrong, but also why running a correction as soon as possible is important. "We correct our mistakes. And it's a very painful thing for us, because we're basically admitting that we failed to do our job," Schmidt said. But admitting errors shows "the devotion that we have to trying to follow the facts and get it right."

WHAT MEDIA SOURCES CAN YOU TRUST?

As you move through the cascade of political information, know that there are media outlets you can feel comfortable trusting and going to first to get the facts. Though some of these are traditional outlets, they of course all have a strong online presence, and nearly anything in print can be found online or on their apps or social media pages.

A warning before I dive in: I know newspapers seem like a thing of the past, but the information they report still drives a majority of coverage, political and otherwise. Making reading a newspaper a habit will make you a better voter in the future. And yes, reading a newspaper on any device counts as reading a newspaper.

A place to start in identifying those trustworthy outlets is its history. "A track record counts for something," CNN's Stelter said. "There's a reason why the Associated Press and the *New York Times* and NBC and ABC and Reuters and other big, old-fashioned news outlets remain among the most trusted. And that's because they've been doing it a long time . . . and they have a reputation for trying to get it right."

The same goes for regional and big-city papers, like the *Houston Chronicle* (founded 1901), the *Omaha World-Herald* (1885), the *Salt Lake Tribune* (1870), and the *Sacramento Bee* (1857). Small-town papers and local radio stations often have similar legacies to these larger outlets, even though most papers are having to do so much more with many fewer subscribers. Local television stations also strive to bring you accurate information, though consider that their national ownership may direct coverage and commentary more than is obvious from watching.

The three major television networks—ABC, NBC, and CBS—are probably the most down-the-middle of national television coverage, and their morning and evening news programs hit the highlights of national stories and high-profile state races. CNN is the most straightforward of the cable news channels.

Best places for nitty-gritty, nearly hour-to-hour fact updates on national races? Newswires like Reuters and the Associated Press. Newswires have people stationed all over the world and provide info to other news organizations. Those organizations send reporters to cover presidential candidates essentially any time they're in public, and have reporters covering the U.S. House and Senate full-time as well. If a candidate said something publicly or did anything new or unusual on the campaign trail, those services are very likely to have the account or will very quickly confirm it.

FactCheck.org is a great place to go for detailed fact-or-fiction breakdowns on controversial statements. Snopes.com is another helpful, nonpartisan fact-checking site.

Podcasts are a great way to listen to news from traditional outlets, news radio like National Public Radio, and experts and commentators on nearly any topic imaginable. Check the hosts' bios and their other work to evaluate both their trustworthiness and any biases.

Focusing on household-name news organizations leaves out countless news sites that provide straightforward, accurate, informative political coverage. But—just like with the bigger ones—it'd be impossible to list them all. If you know how to evaluate a news story—whether it comes to you online, in print, via video, or in your earbuds—you'll be able to figure out what and who you can trust.

WHY IS READING THE NEWS SO IMPORTANT?

Many sources—the candidates' websites and speeches, partisan commentators, activist organizations—provide information that supports their candidate of choice, and it's worthwhile to take those in, too. But the reason it's so important to read unbiased news sources is they're giving you the full picture: what the candidates want you to know and sometimes what they wish you didn't. It allows you to evaluate how those things match with what you believe without someone telling you how to feel. Getting the full picture is a crucial part of your superpower as a voter.

The more politically aware you are and the more you trust the reputable news media, according to research, the better you are at telling fact from opinion. Americans who had "high political awareness" and placed "high levels of trust in the news media" were much more likely to be able to tell factual news statements from opinion statements, a Pew study found. (Digital savvy was a big indicator, too.)

DIVERSIFY, DIVERSIFY

Most people's media diet consists at least in part of outlets or reporters that tend to support their points of view. Americans are increasingly likely to gravitate to news and information that aligns with the political positions they already have, both by selecting it on their own and by social media services' algorithms prioritizing it in their feeds.

But it's important to diversify the news you read, watch, and listen to, and to be aware that hyperpartisan (only interested in supporting the political right or left) rhetoric can be misleading.

In the lead-up to the 2016 election, a BuzzFeed News analysis found that hyper-partisan Facebook pages regularly trafficked in false information, and that false information found its way to many people:

The review of more than 1,000 posts from six large hyperpartisan Facebook pages selected from the right and from the left also found that the least accurate pages generated some of the highest numbers of shares, reactions, and comments on Facebook—far more than the three large mainstream political news pages analyzed for comparison.

Our analysis of three hyperpartisan right-wing Facebook pages found that 38% of all posts were either a mixture of true and false or mostly false, compared to 19% of posts from three hyperpartisan left-wing pages that were either a mixture of true and false or mostly false.

I'm not saying to never look at sites or channels that report their news in a way that conforms to your views—following people whose opinions you trust is part of forming an understanding of issues. The key is making sure they are honest and accurate, and keeping that information as only a slice of your news diet. Take in information you agree with, information that's down the middle, and information you disagree with, too.

NON-NEWS SOURCES

When it comes to evaluating a candidate, there are non-news sources that also help you learn more. Here are some examples:

- **The candidates' own websites**

They help you know what the candidate prioritizes and what they see as their strengths.

Candidates' websites usually lay out their positions on prominent issues and the plans they hope to enact if elected.

They're also the place to learn if candidates are hosting meet and greets or town halls where you can hear their views and possibly ask questions.

- **The League of Women Voters' Vote411.org**

It has details about voting deadlines and procedures in your state.

The site includes questionnaires where candidates for a particular office are all asked the same questions, including topics specific to their region.

It also highlights ballot initiatives as deserving extra attention before a person votes.

- **Candidate debates**

Presidential candidate debates obviously get the most attention, but debates are held for many other offices, too—congressional, state legislature, and mayoral races included.

Consider in advance of the debate what issues you most care about so you're listening closely for comments and questions related to them.

- **Research sites and organizations that focus on topics that interest you**

If it's an organization you trust, it can be a great way to help crystallize your thinking on issues.

Many issues sites will take a position, so just be sure to confirm and understand who's paying for the site, said the League's Jeanette Senecal. Ask yourself, "Who is trying to influence my understanding of a candidate or that issue?"

Again, that last comment is the central question to ask yourself about any information, news or otherwise, you come across. Know who is behind their information and what their goal is. Be an educated voter. And like getting a second opinion on a medical diagnosis, when it comes to information about candidates and issues, it's always good to check a second source.

THINK BEFORE YOU SHARE

Questions to ask about any piece of information online before you share it yourself:

What is the source of the info?

- The source is where the information originated. Did it come from an individual? A news organization? An advocate for something? In the words of a teacher I heard worrying about her middle-school students' reading habits: "Google isn't a source!"

- If it's a news organization, is it one you know?

- If it's a person (or a news outlet) you're unfamiliar with, find out where they got the information. Were they there? Did they get the information from someone there? Did they read it somewhere?

- If the source is someone or something you don't know, click on it and learn more. If you still can't tell if it's trustworthy, ignore it.

If you aren't certain of the source, don't share.

Do you have the link?

- If so, click on it and make sure it says what you think it says.

- If you don't have it or it's not a trusted source, find a story from a trusted news source with the same information.

If you don't have the link, don't share.

Have you read more than the headline?

- Headlines are not the news. Headlines are like a preview of a television drama. It gives you an idea of what the story is about, but it's no substitute for watching the whole thing. If you've read only the headline, you don't know the story.

If you've only read the headline, don't share.

Are you looking at the original post?

• If it's a screen grab, such as of an article or tweet, find the original. Social media handles, logos, and avatars are easy to fake. Very knowledgeable people get tricked all the time.

If it's a screen grab, don't share without confirming its accuracy.

Is the headline describing facts,
or is it trying to change your mind?

• News stories can have clever headlines, but they shouldn't read like they're trying to convince you of something.

• If it is trying to convince you of something—about someone's "ridiculous" plan or someone's "brilliant" plan—read it with that in mind. The facts might still be correct, but know it's coming at you with a point of view.

If it's something that's trying to convince people of something, note that when you share.

Does the story present multiple points of view?

• A news story should always describe the different takes on an issue, and provide context.

If a story is one-sided, either don't share, or note that issue when you do share.

Does it sound too good to be true?
Too juicy, too outrageous?

- See if more than one trustworthy news outlet has it. If it's big news, multiple media organizations will try to confirm the story quickly.

If only one outlet has something, consider waiting to share.

UNDERSTANDING POLLING

During election periods, you'll hear nonstop chatter about polls. Polls are regularly released that tell us which candidates are thought to be ahead and which issues voters care about.

Polls give an idea of what a larger group thinks about something by asking a smaller portion of that group. A poll might ask 1,000 American kids ages eight to twelve their favorite movie from last year to help determine what all American kids ages eight to twelve think was the best movie last year.

You might wonder how asking a fairly small number of kids gives you a good idea of what all American kids think. Philip Bump, a *Washington Post* reporter who focuses on data and polls, describes it this way: you only need one spoonful of soup to know if the whole bowl is too hot.

POLLING JARGON: REPRESENTATIVE SAMPLE

Representative sample: the characteristics of a group of people polled needs to match the characteristics of the larger group whose opinion you're trying to figure out.

A very important aspect of polling is that the group polled is a representative sample of the larger group. It won't work if you taste your mac and cheese to see if your soup is too hot!

That same idea is true for political polling. If the people designing a poll are trying to find out U.S. citizens' preferred presidential candidate—meaning they want to predict how most of the country will vote—they can't just ask people from one of the candidate's home states, or only people from New York City, which usually votes for Democrats, or from rural Alabama, which usually favors Republicans.

You have to find the right mix of people—enough Republicans, enough Democrats, enough independents, enough people from all different parts of the country, and many other factors.

WHY DOES POLITICAL POLLING MATTER?

It might seem reasonable to just ignore polls, but candidates, voters, and news organizations use them to make big decisions.

• Candidates use them to decide which issues to focus on, to understand what voters in their area might want, and to decide what political ads to make.

• News organizations use them to help them understand what readers are interested in, and because leaders in polls often get more coverage, polls impact the news, too.

• Voters and political organizations use them to decide who to give money to, and campaigns need money to succeed.

HOW TO READ POLITICAL POLLS

Around election time, the two types of numbers you're most likely to see are candidates' current predicted share of the vote and candidates' current chance of winning. Those numbers can be very different, and it's important to know which one you're seeing.

POLITICAL JARGON: HORSE RACE

Horse race: a term that has been used to describe political contests since the nineteenth century. It mostly refers to a close race between two candidates. A presidential race is often called the "horse race" between the candidates.

For example, the percentage of voters expected to vote for each of the candidates (in a two-person race) might look something like this:

Candidate A: 48 percent
Candidate B: 52 percent

But the candidates' percentage chances of winning might look something like this:

Candidate A: 30 percent
Candidate B: 70 percent

- Note: Often these "chance of winning" numbers come from organizations that create an average of polls. It is not just a simple average, though; they use complicated formulas, including giving the most reliable polls more weight than others.

How is it possible that the numbers in the two types of polls would be so different? Because if a candidate gets 52 percent of the vote on Election Day, they'll win. So, if there's a good chance they'll get that majority of the votes, then they have a good chance of winning the election.

But it's really important not to confuse the two types of numbers: it's still a pretty close race if there is only a few points' difference in the percentage of people expected to vote for the candidate. A swing of a percentage point or two would make a very big difference in that "chance of winning" number. Also, an 80 percent chance of winning is not 100 percent. If someone told you there was a 20 percent chance something really bad would happen if you opened a particular door, you'd probably keep it closed.

VOTING TIP:

The most important advice about voting and polling? Never let your candidate's supposed chance of winning or losing keep you from voting. THE ONLY POLL THAT REALLY MATTERS IS HOW VOTERS VOTE ON ELECTION DAY!

MORE IMPORTANT THINGS TO NOTICE ABOUT ELECTION POLLS AND PERCENTAGES

- If you see a number about a candidate, always look for the other numbers.

 If 50 percent of those who answered poll questions support Candidate A, you need to know how many support Candidate B. They could be tied, or 25 percent could support Candidate B and 25 percent could be undecided.

- Check the "margin of error."

 The "margin of error" is how many percentage points the poll knows the number could be off. Usually the number applies to each candidate individually. It's normal for polls to have one—polling is not an exact science.

 If Candidate A has 47 percent of the vote, Candidate B has 42 percent (leaving room for people who haven't made up their minds), and the poll has a 3 percent margin of error.

Candidate A might actually have 50 percent or 44 percent. Candidate B could have 45 percent or 39 percent.

The 3 percent margin of error means they could be tied, or Candidate B could even be in the lead.

• Polling extra credit

Look at more than one poll to see if they have similar results.

Check back to see how the numbers have moved when new polls are released.

DON'T JUDGE A POLL (ONLY) BY ITS NUMBERS

Now that we're clear on how to think about the numbers, we're all good with polls, right? Of course not! You also need to think about who conducted the poll, and how they did it. It's similar to evaluating a news story's trustworthiness: Do you recognize the name of the company that published the poll? Did they show their work by explaining how many people were polled, who they were, and how the people were contacted? Did they explain exactly what they asked?

WHO IS POLLED IN POLITICAL RACES?

• Poll takers try to predict who will vote—they don't want to talk to someone who is never going to go to the polls.

- In earlier stages of an election, they might talk to people who are registered to vote.

- As an election gets closer, it's narrowed to likely voters.

A note of caution: because it's never certain who will actually vote—a "likely voter" might decide to stay home—poll conductors always say they're only giving you a snapshot in time, rather than predicting who will win.

Names like Pew and Gallup and large, mainstream news organizations are among those considered trustworthy polling organizations. It's not that smaller places can't conduct good polls, it's just that conducting proper polls is very pricey and takes a lot of time.

If you don't recognize the organization, look it up to see if it has a particular focus, angle, or specialty. You might not recognize the name Kaiser, for example, but the Kaiser Family Foundation website tells you it's a nonprofit that focuses on health care. Whether the organization releasing the poll is left-leaning or right-leaning is another thing to think about—it doesn't mean the poll isn't trustworthy, but it does mean they're hoping the information will convince you of something. (To determine an organization's political leanings, see how they describe themselves, and then search to see how a prominent newspaper or news site has described them.)

HOW PEOPLE ARE REACHED FOR POLLS

• Live telephone calls

Believe it or not, many polls are still conducted via live telephone calls, where a person working for the polling organization speaks directly to the person being polled. It's considered one of the most reliable methods.

As you might expect, it's become much harder to conduct polls this way because people don't answer their phones when they don't know who is calling. (And it's really tough to reach young voters this way.)

• Interactive Voice Response or "IVR" calls

This is where a caller picks up and hears a recorded voice that asks them questions and tells them to respond via pressing a number on their phone.

These can still be reliable, but are less preferred than live-person calls.

• Online

More and more polls are being conducted online, but it still involves the polling organization choosing the people to poll so they make sure they have the right mix of people.

Warning: if you can choose to respond to an online poll yourself, it might be fun, but it's not a reliable way to find how a broader group feels.

LOOK AT WHAT THE PEOPLE CARE ABOUT

Many polling experts argue that focusing only on candidate-versus-candidate polls results in missing the bigger picture. Karlyn Bowman, an expert on public polling and a data analyst at the right-leaning public policy research organization American Enterprise Institute, prefers polls that ask about issues because they take the specific candidates out of the equation and show what is really on the minds of the American people.

Gallup has regularly asked Americans the same open-ended question since 1935: What do you think is the most important problem facing this country today? Polls like that "are really much more concerned about ordinary life, about what makes America tick," Bowman said.

A GLANCE AT AMERICA'S "MOST IMPORTANT PROBLEMS"

A *New York Times* interactive story showed how much the answers to the Gallup poll questions reflect the era. Below are some of Americans' top concerns over time.

1935: unemployment

America was going through the Great Depression, a time when many Americans struggled to earn enough money to pay for food or housing.

1965: civil rights and race relations

President Johnson's famous civil rights speech was in March 1965.

Polls are not perfect, but their ability to tell us more about ourselves is what makes them important in the overall political landscape, Bowman said. "They help us understand what a very complex and [diverse] public is thinking or not thinking about a lot of different issues, and I think that's really important in our democracy."

POLLS AND THE 2016 ELECTION

I met my friends Emily and Amy for a pizza lunch on Election Day 2016. We chatted about how the country was most likely twelve hours away from electing a woman as president of the United States. Why did we (and nearly everyone else) think that? Expert after expert was saying Hillary Clinton's chance of winning was over 80 percent.

That 80 percent chance of a Clinton win began looking

iffy early on Election Night; by early morning the chance was zero. And it took zero seconds for people to wonder how polls got it so very wrong.

While poll takers and analysts certainly couldn't say they got it exactly right, they spent much of the immediate election aftermath saying they weren't so wrong, either. They tried to drive home that a close race is a close race and that an 80 percent chance of winning still means a very real chance of losing.

Top professors, journalists, professional polling organizations, and others who evaluate election-related polls got together to look into what happened, and wrote a big report of their findings. Here's what they said:

- **The national polls weren't so wrong.**

  These are the polls that looked at how the country would vote as a whole.

  Those polls said Clinton had about a 3 percentage point lead; she won the popular vote by 2 percentage points.

- **State polls had a historically bad year.**

  State polls look at which candidate is likely to win that state.

  State polls said Clinton had a narrow lead in Michigan, Pennsylvania, and Wisconsin, but Donald

Trump ended up winning all three. Those three states decided the election.

- **A few major factors caused the state polls to be off.**

An unusually high number of people made up their minds or changed their minds very late, and an unusually high number of those people voted for the same candidate (Trump).

The polls included too many college-educated voters and not enough non–college-educated voters, and those conducting the polls did not adjust their calculations properly.

That turned out to be a huge factor in the race. In general, people with a higher level of education voted for Clinton.

This is something polls are trying very hard to do better on in future elections.

WHAT IS THE ELECTORAL COLLEGE?

To be a true voter-in-the-know, you need to be aware of the Electoral College.

"Electoral College" may sound like a school for elections, but it's not an actual place. It's how the Constitution says the president must be chosen. In this case, "college" means an organized group with a particular duty.

Americans who vote in a presidential election don't officially choose the president. The Electoral College does. When Americans vote for president, what they're really doing is telling the Electoral College which candidate to choose.

If you think that's strange . . . it kind of is. The United States' Electoral College system is unique among democracies.

Electors: The people of the Electoral College who choose the president.

538: The total number of electors.

They are distributed among the states based on the state's number of congressional seats plus two. (Two for the number of senators each state has.)

Washington, D.C., also gets electoral votes.

270: The total number of electoral votes a person needs to win the presidency.

55: The number of electoral votes of California, the state with the largest population.

3: The number of electoral votes that Washington, D.C., and the states with the smallest populations have. For the states, it represents their two senators plus their one member of the U.S. House of Representatives.

HOW DOES THE ELECTORAL COLLEGE WORK?

On Election Night, you can watch on TV or online as all the votes are added up. But you'll see that the news is showing a nationwide vote count (the "popular vote"), and also announcing when a candidate "wins" a particular state. Winning states is what really matters.

In forty-eight states, whichever candidate gets the most popular votes wins all of that state's Electoral

College votes. So whichever candidate gets the most votes in California gets all fifty-five electoral votes, even if it's a close race. It doesn't matter if a candidate wins those forty-eight states by 2,000 votes or two million. If they win, they win all the Electoral College votes.

THE ELECTION OF 1800

Originally, there was not a separate ballot for president and vice president, so the person who won the most Electoral College votes was president and the second-place winner vice president. In the 1800 election, presidential candidate Thomas Jefferson and running-mate Aaron Burr ran against incumbent John Adams.

When the Electoral College voted, Jefferson and Burr tied. Battling loyalties meant some preferred Burr, and it took a week and thirty-six rounds of votes in the House of Representatives to sort things out. Jefferson became president with Burr as vice president after Alexander Hamilton supported Jefferson. The 1800 election led to the Constitution's Twelfth Amendment, which requires separate votes for president and vice president.

In Maine and Nebraska, the two states that aren't "winner-take-all," the popular vote winner gets two electoral votes, and the rest go to the candidate who won the popular vote in each of the state's congressional districts. Unlike California or Texas with their dozens of congressional districts, Maine has only two districts and Nebraska three. So, while they're outliers in how they calculate their Electoral College votes, neither state has played a deciding role in a presidential race.

WHEN DO THE ELECTORS VOTE?

Even this part sounds complicated. The designated day is the first Monday after the second Wednesday of December. In 2016, that meant December 19. In 2020, it is December 14. The electors meet in person to vote, usually in their respective state capitals.

WHO ARE THE ELECTORS?

Electors change with every election. The parties in each state choose a slate of potential electors, and then, in the general election, when voters vote for their candidate, they are also voting for their state's electors.

States have their own methods for choosing electors, but they are often selected by members of the state's political party at that party's state convention. They can't be current members of the U.S. House of Representatives or Senate.

Usually the electors are chosen as a sort of reward for loyalty and service to the political party, or maybe because they have an affiliation with the presidential candidate. (Bill Clinton was a New York delegate for Hillary.)

Both Republicans and Democrats have their own electors, though the electors for the candidates who didn't win in that particular state aren't needed.

HOW DOES THE VOTING WORK EXACTLY?

The vote itself is uneventful and predictable. It's why after Election Day the presidential candidate who is projected the winner is immediately referred to as the president elect. Electors are like "mirrors," law professor and constitutional law expert Sanford Levinson said. They are expected to vote for the state's popular vote winner. Electors are generally chosen for their loyalty, so they almost always vote for who they are expected to vote for.

POLITICAL JARGON: FAITHLESS ELECTOR

Faithless elector: An elector who votes for someone other than the state popular vote winner. In the 2016 election, for instance, a few electors voted for John Kasich, the former governor of Ohio, instead of Clinton or Trump.

What happens when someone is a "faithless elector"?

- Not much. Some states have laws requiring their electors to vote for the state popular vote winner, but punishments for not following are minimal, if there are any at all. Many states do not "bind" their electors to vote for the popular vote winner.

- The Supreme Court is scheduled to hear a case in 2020 over whether states have the right to bind their electors and require them to choose the state popular vote winner. A decision is expected before the 2020 election.

THE ELECTION OF 1824

Four serious contenders for president led to an Electoral College debacle in 1824. Andrew Jackson won the most Electoral College votes, but not enough to win the presidency. The fourth-place Electoral College finisher, Henry Clay, "eagerly assumed the role of kingmaker," Norman Ornstein wrote in *After the People Vote: A Guide to the Electoral College*. Clay met with fellow candidate John Quincy Adams, and there may or may not have been an agreement that Clay would be secretary of state if he delivered the votes of Ohio and Kentucky, which Clay had won, to Adams. Clay denied there was any such agreement, but Adams became president and Clay indeed became secretary of state.

WHY IS THE ELECTORAL COLLEGE CONTROVERSIAL?

Some people think that the popular vote should choose the president. That it shouldn't matter, in other words, how state citizens vote, but instead only how the country's citizens vote as a whole. For most U.S. elections in history, the popular vote winner and the Electoral College were the same. Only five times in history have the Electoral College and popular vote winners been different. You've been hearing a lot more about the Electoral College lately because two of those times were recent.

- **2016:** Clinton beat Trump in the popular vote by about 3 million votes, but Trump won the Electoral College.

  It came down to the Electoral College votes in Michigan, Pennsylvania, and Wisconsin. Trump won those states by about 80,000 total votes, so he also won their Electoral College votes and the presidency.

- **2000:** Al Gore beat George W. Bush in the popular vote, but Bush won the Electoral College and became president.

  After losing the Supreme Court battle over a recount of Florida's votes, and thus that state's Electoral College votes, Vice President Gore had to oversee the official Electoral College count in his role as president of the Senate. Bush took the oath of office three weeks later.

WHY DO WE HAVE THE ELECTORAL COLLEGE?

The Electoral College was created at the 1787 Constitutional Convention in Philadelphia. Experts disagree on many aspects of why the founders chose this method for presidential elections, but one reason most get behind is a practical one.

While the idea of a popular vote was suggested, the

drafters were concerned that the country wouldn't have an opportunity to learn enough about the candidates. In the 1780s, there was no system of mass communication. No internet! No radio! Newspapers did exist, but they were mostly local. Travel was too difficult for the candidates to go everywhere and meet citizens, and information moved too slowly from place to place.

Plus, counting and reporting the popular vote would have taken months and involved a lot of uncertainty and challenges.

This method was also meant to put distance between the executive and legislative branches by making sure that the president wasn't selected by legislators, the way the prime minister is chosen in Britain's parliamentary system. The founders wanted the presidency to be a separate branch of government, and for lawmakers to select him or her only in the case of a tie in the Electoral College.

The certainty among experts on why the Electoral College was created doesn't extend too much beyond this. Some believe it was a way to save the country from a bad selection.

Here's an explanation from founder Alexander Hamilton. In one of the Federalist Papers (essays sent to newspapers to encourage states to approve the

Constitution), Hamilton discusses the Electoral College, saying the electors will perform one job, and that's assemble "and vote for some fit person as President." The Electoral College, Hamilton wrote,

affords a moral certainty, that the office of President will never fall to the lot of any man who is not . . . endowed with the requisite qualifications. Talents for low intrigue, and the little arts of popularity, may alone suffice to elevate a man . . . in a single State; but it will require other talents, and a different kind of merit, to establish him in the esteem and confidence of the whole Union.

In other words: even if someone unqualified gets chosen just because they're popular, the Electoral College can fix the problem.

This seems like clear evidence of where the founders stood. But Hamilton was in salesman mode, urging adoption of the Constitution, and some prominent experts think he could have been finding a compelling reason that went beyond the framers' reasoning at the time they created it.

There is even disagreement over whether the Electoral College was set up to keep founders from slaveholding states happy. In a popular vote system, the larger number of eligible voters in Northern states meant Southern candidates were likely to be shut out. But the South's population was much greater than its number of eligible voters—it was also home to many slaves. In an Electoral College system based on population rather than the number of eligible voters, things would be more even between the North and South. In the end, enslaved people counted as three-fifths of a person.

But it's debatable whether this benefit for slaveholding states was a driving factor to create the Electoral College. "The electoral college," said historian Alexander Keyssar, "imported the compromises on slavery that had already been reached dealing with congressional representation. In that sense it did reward slaveholders, but I don't think it was the point of this particular weird institution."

INSIDE ONE 2016 ELECTORAL COLLEGE VOTE

More than thirty electors from around the state of Texas gathered in the main legislative chamber of the mammoth pink limestone state capitol building in Austin on December 19, 2016. The observation gallery was full, the lights twinkled on a two-story Christmas tree, and both sunlight and shouts of protesters streamed in from outside. After a local girls' choir sang the national anthem and a reverend said a prayer, the Texas secretary of state called roll, one elector at a time. The electors responded with a mix of "here" and "present," but when the name Art Sisneros was called, there was silence.

After a lot of soul-searching, Republican elector Sisneros, a welding supply salesman from Liberty County, had decided several weeks earlier he couldn't in good conscience vote for Trump and would resign his elector position. (Sisneros's fellow citizens in Liberty County—the very "red" county where I grew up—made clear how they expected him to vote. Trump received 78 percent of the vote in Liberty County.)

So, what happened? Electors are so important that the Constitution insists they choose the president, so was there a full-out crisis in the state of Texas? Nope. The electors voted, with little fanfare, to replace Sisneros with a woman from another small town in the same congressional district who was happy to vote for Trump.

All the electors voted by secret ballot. As it turned out, two other electors refused to follow the party line. One voted for longtime Texas representative Ron Paul and one for Ohio's John Kasich.

But the other thirty-six electors chose Trump, and an official announced Trump had enough electoral votes to be named president. The gallery cheered.

WHY DO WE STILL HAVE THE ELECTORAL COLLEGE?

Whatever the reasons the framers created the Electoral College, the practical ones no longer apply. Citizens have immediate access to an endless amount of information about the candidates. We don't have to worry as much about states completing and reporting their presidential vote counts.

States' rights and population concerns do still dominate arguments about why we should keep the Electoral College. If the presidential race were decided by popular vote, the argument goes, candidates would spend all their time in New York and Los Angeles and Houston and Chicago recruiting the millions of voters in those cities, and, once the primaries were over, never step foot in the cornfields of Iowa. The Electoral College, in other words, gives smaller states a say.

And that might be true. But as it stands, once the primary elections are over, candidates mostly just stealthily stop by the biggest cities to raise money and then spend all their time in swing states, none of which are home to the millions of citizens in New York, Los Angeles, Houston, or Chicago.

POLITICAL JARGON: SWING AND BATTLEGROUND

"Swing states" or "battleground states": states whose popular vote outcomes aren't so predictable. Their popular vote might go to a Democratic candidate in one election and a Republican the next, which means their Electoral College votes are up for grabs.

In the 2016 presidential election, only a few states were won by less than 2 percent. Clinton won New Hampshire and Minnesota. Trump won Florida, Michigan, Pennsylvania, and Wisconsin. As noted above, Michigan, Pennsylvania, and Wisconsin decided the election.

PROPOSALS TO END THE ELECTORAL COLLEGE

A week after the 2016 election, U.S. Senator Barbara Boxer of California proposed a constitutional amendment to abolish the Electoral College. It was far from the first such plan. Over time, there have been more than 700 proposals to abolish or modify the Electoral College process, according to FairVote.

The only real way to alter or end the Electoral College is to amend the Constitution. That's extremely difficult to do under the best of circumstances, and impossible in a divided political climate.

Remember that to amend the Constitution, both the Senate and House must approve the change by a two-thirds vote, and three-fourths of states must agree as well. As of early 2020, the last amendment was in 1992 and involved congressional pay. Before that was 1971, when the voting age was lowered to eighteen.

Both the House and the Senate have separately passed bills to end or dramatically change the Electoral College. But they've never wanted to do it at the same time, as would be required to pass an amendment and send it to the states for approval.

THE ELECTION OF 1876

The election of 1876 was ugly. Republican candidate Rutherford B. Hayes's campaign accused Samuel Tilden of being a drunkard and a swindler. Tilden's side said Hayes had stolen from dead soldiers and shot his own mother. Tilden received more popular votes, and was only one vote shy of the number of Electoral College votes he needed with several states still counting.

The story goes that the national Republican Party leaders put pressure on those states, telegramming them to say if their state went for Hayes, Hayes would win. The national Republican Party chairman then claimed Hayes had won, and it became a huge mess.

President Ulysses Grant sent troops to keep the peace as the votes were actually counted, and accusations of cheating flew. The dispute lasted until March 1877. Eventually Hayes was named president. Tilden believed until his dying day he should have been president.

One of the compromises to end this dispute was that the North pull all its troops out of the South. It signaled the end to Reconstruction and many of the political gains of African Americans in the South.

SMALL STATES, SWING STATES, AND THE ELECTORAL COLLEGE

Both smaller states and swing states benefit from an outsize power because of the Electoral College, and that power earns them a lot of attention from lawmakers and candidates.

In 2000, George Bush got nine Electoral College votes by winning Wyoming and North and South Dakota. Al Gore got five votes by winning New Mexico. New Mexico had roughly the same population as the other three states combined. It's a vivid, if selective, example of the difference it makes giving small states like North and South Dakota and Wyoming an Electoral College boost their population numbers don't alone warrant, Levinson said.

Florida and Ohio, considered swing states in presidential elections, have much larger populations and Electoral College representations, and thus also see the extra benefits and attention by being high-stakes, multi-visit states for candidates.

As some states inch closer to battleground status, it's in the current majority party's interest to keep the Electoral College. Texas's state house is 55 percent Republican, and the state voted 52 percent for Trump in 2016. The current majority party would have no reason to lessen its Electoral College power by allowing the 3.9 million Texans' votes that went for Clinton to actually contribute to the outcome.

The bottom line is that some states would have to give up some of the power and clout the Electoral College gives them, and states don't like to do that.

THE POPULAR VOTE PACT

Citizens who would like to move to a popular vote system aren't completely stuck, though it does still come down to how their state feels. In recent years, multiple states have signed into law the National Popular Vote Interstate Compact, which would require those states' electoral votes to go to the winner of the nationwide popular vote.

But there's a catch. The compact doesn't go into effect until enough states have passed it that their electoral votes combine to add up to 270. States don't want to risk giving away their electoral votes unless others are doing the same. Maryland became the first state to pass the compact in 2007. In total, fifteen states and Washington, D.C., have joined. When Oregon joined in 2019, the states in the compact had a combined 196 electoral votes.

One thing to keep in mind: it's an untested system, so it's not clear what would happen if a state that had joined the compact backed out after an election. Unknowns aside, the compact is a simpler approach than trying to amend the Constitution, even if it still has a ways to go before enough states pass it.

THE WHOLE POINT OF IT ALL: SHOWING UP TO VOTE MATTERS

So, how should you think about the Electoral College

when you get to vote? Well, if you live in a battleground state, the candidates visit you a lot for a reason. Your vote is especially sought after in presidential races and could help determine a close election.

And if you live in a state that's already pretty red or pretty blue? First, the most important elections aren't always at the top of the ballot. Your school board members impact every student in your community. Your mayor and city council members make decisions that touch your life every day. Your state representatives govern your health care and your voting rights, and may draw your U.S. congressional district lines. And the Electoral College has nothing to do with how you choose your U.S. representatives and senators.

Even if you're likely to be in the minority in your state's presidential race, it's still vital that you vote every time you can. Candidates should know where state citizens stand. They are there to serve you, even if you don't always agree with them or they with you. Voters for the losing party still have influence, especially if their numbers are mighty.

Plus, we are far from 100 percent turnout, which means there's room for improvement and increased voting power at every age group, racial group, and income level. But that's especially true for groups with lower turnout rates, including young people, Latinx, and Asian Americans. In some races, even moderate increases in turnout can decide the election.

So get to the polls and recruit people to join you.

PART THREE

HOW TO GET PEOPLE TO VOTE

YOUNG PEOPLE AND VOTING

My mom had me tag along on election days. We would park in the library's circular drive and I'd prepare myself for the blast of freezing Texas air-conditioning. Mom would chat with poll workers, I'd listen closely for any good gossip, and then she'd fill out her ballot.

In our small town it took no more than ten minutes, and it seemed like no big deal at the time. But now I understand: she taught me to be a voter.

My mom was doing something countless voting advocates—both those with famous names and those regular, concerned citizens in our communities—are trying to do on a grand scale: convince young people of the importance of voting and show them how to do it.

On a pretty Los Angeles morning in 2018, *Grey's Anatomy* and *Scandal* television show creator and general Hollywood big shot Shonda Rhimes told an audience of 10,000 young women that "if you want your voice to be represented, if you want your face to be represented," you need to vote. That afternoon, youthful former staffers for President Barack Obama previewed their *Pod Save America* HBO special at a historic theater in nearby Glendale, including a video on how to best get out the vote. The next morning, teenage TV star Yara Shahidi gathered more than 100 young activists at a bright and open office near the Los Angeles airport to brainstorm how to recruit their peers to go to the polls.

A few weeks later, at the storied Cooper Union building in New York City, where suffragists once lobbied for women's right to vote, volunteers gathered as they headed into the final weekend before the November 2018 midterms. Those who had called potential voters and gone door-to-door to remind people to vote were rewarded with a pep talk by the *Avengers* franchise star Mark Ruffalo.

Efforts like this made a difference.

Voting advocates hope that ramping up the get-out-the-vote methods from 2018 leads to record turnout in 2020. In our very online world, making a personal connection is still the most effective method to get someone to vote. The idea is this: harness the modern tools of social media to employ the age-old tactic of peer pressure to get friends, both online and in real life, to complete the analog act of voting. Voting can be the good kind of trendy.

FOCUS ON YOUNG PEOPLE

A top priority for anyone who cares about voter turnout is seeing more young people vote.

The message of those who preach the power of voting to young people is this: First, voting is the best way to make your opinion matter. What are you most passionate about—climate change, gun control, health care, women's reproductive rights, immigration reform, corruption . . . ? Vote for the candidates who support your causes.

Second, it's empowering. You're making a difference.

Third, it's one of the most meaningful things you can do with your friends.

How do you convince a person to vote for the first time? It requires answering any questions or worries about the process, from how to register to learning about candidates to finding where to vote.

Movements to increase the youth vote started decades ago. Adults close to you likely remember the start of the Rock the Vote campaign, founded in 1990 and still going strong.

Shortly before performing at a 2018 "Party at the Polls" voting event in Nashville, rock star and get-out-the-vote veteran Sheryl Crow talked youth turnout as one of her two preteen sons played with instruments nearby. Crow planned to take her sons with her to vote.

She worked with Rock the Vote shortly after its start and later toured with the Beastie Boys on a Rock the Vote tour. She's among the activists who hope today's current youth movement is stronger than ever. She'd felt there was momentum in the past, she said, but now she sees a new importance: "This feels as though we're at a turning point."

MORE PARTYING AT THE POLLS

Organizations weren't the only ones who stepped up their voting efforts in 2018. Companies did, too. Endeavor is an entertainment and media company that works with clients including the singer Rihanna, actress Emma Stone, and actor Dwayne "The Rock" Johnson. It set a goal of 100 percent voter registration for its eligible employees, and found a way to encourage music fans to vote, too. Shortly before the 2018 midterm elections, the company sponsored a free morning concert with Crow, singer-songwriter Billy Ray Cyrus, Grammy winner Jason Isbell, and the Highwomen singer Amanda Shires, among others. Attendees then took a ten-minute walk—a brass band playing as they marched—to line up to vote early.

WHAT MOVED YOUNG VOTERS IN 2018

Disliking the candidates and issues was the top reason young registered voters gave for not voting in 2016, showing that campaigns are having trouble connecting with and motivating them.

But that election was before the February 2017 shooting at Marjory Stoneman Douglas High School in

Parkland, Florida. The hugely visible and deeply emotional demand for gun reform by a group of the school's students became a movement. As we'll talk about later, they founded March for Our Lives in part to encourage voter recruitment efforts.

YOUTH VOTERS AND GUN SAFETY

Before the 2018 election:

- 77 percent of young people who said they planned to vote said gun control would be an important issue in determining their vote.

- 64 percent of all young people favor stricter gun control laws in the United States, fifteen points higher than six years before.

Voting organizations want young people to learn a crucial fact: the more you vote, the more politicians pay attention to your issues. Paul Gronke, the Oregon-based professor, is straightforward with his students: they have problems getting their student loan concerns addressed, he explains, but his benefits and taxes are always a priority for politicians. Guess why? he asks. "Because I vote all the time and you don't."

In other words, older people are generally the ones who take voting seriously and get what they want. But it doesn't have to be that way.

Those who work to register high schoolers often emphasize the political influence young voters could have. Hannah Mixdorf, who helps lead youth voting organization Inspire2Vote, makes sure students know that Americans eighteen to twenty-nine years old make up a huge voting group in the United States, but vote at the lowest rate. She encourages them to see their potential: "Imagine the power you'd have if this entire generation of voters mobilized and cast a ballot."

SPEAKING YOUR LANGUAGE

The country needs young people to care about voting, but it also needs to earn that enthusiasm—to show why it's relevant, to explain how to do it, and to use language that young people can relate to.

All of those factors came together at Yara Shahidi's 2018 We Vote Next summit held at the TOMS shoes headquarters in Los Angeles. Shahidi is an actress on ABC's hit show *Black-ish*, and stars in and produces its spin-off, *Grown-ish*. She has more than four million Instagram followers, is a favorite cover girl of glossy magazines and their online components, and attends Harvard University. Oprah Winfrey predicted she'll be president someday. When Barbie introduced a Yara doll in celebration of its sixtieth anniversary in 2019, the doll was wearing a T-shirt that read "VOTE" in multicolored letters.

WE VOTE NEXT

In early 2018, Shahidi appeared on *The Late Show with Stephen Colbert* and told him her upcoming eighteenth-birthday celebration would be a "voting party," where'd she get her friends to register to vote. Her organization, which started as Eighteen x 18 but is planning to go by "We Vote Next" going into 2020, is the pumped-up version of that idea. She's created a community focused on educating young people about voting and mobilizing them to political participation. In general, she wants to make it "the slightest bit easier for our generation to vote," she said at the We Vote Next conference. The group's Instagram feed provides voter registration tips and information nearly daily, including a heads-up about city, state, and special elections.

But Shahidi pushes the big-picture importance of voting, too, working to convince her peers that failing to raise their voices through voting means giving up control of their generation's destiny. Gathering teen thought leaders together is one way she does it, knowing they'll also spread the message to their own online and real-life communities.

We Vote Next attendees were welcomed by five-foot-tall yellow-and-white signs highlighting 100 years of voting history. It went from 1913's "Women March for Voting Rights" to 2013's "A Step Backwards" describing the U.S. Supreme Court's *Shelby County* Voting Rights Act decision. More than 100 excited and casually dressed teenagers and younger twentysomethings milled about in a grassy courtyard topped with white picnic tables, a beanbag game, and a small tent to create voting-inspired pins.

The official participants, called delegates, were from all fifty states and chosen because they'd shown motivation as activists in their communities. Among them was a young woman who'd worked as a page at the Iowa Senate; a Colorado man who would, in 2019, become one of the youngest ever elected to the Denver school board; a female Somali refugee living in Utah; and teenager Auli'i Cravalho, the voice of Disney's Moana and a native Hawaiian concerned about the environment.

Delegates laughed as they jumped into an enclosed yellow slide that delivered them from the second floor to the lobby. At the bottom were pretend voting booths with "ballots" asking which issues they were most passionate about. Hanging throughout the space were signs with voting-related vocabulary, like one for "swing states" above hanging yarn-covered swings.

"When you look at voting as an actual activity,"

Shahidi told the group in her opening address, "often-times it's created as an upper-middle-class hobby. It's [something you do] if you have the time—if you don't have an hourly job, if you have the ability to stand in line and that time works out for you, if your family isn't dependent on your presence somewhere else."

She urged her peers to understand that policy discussions are debates about issues directly affecting their lives, and young people should influence those discussions. "This is a moment to be in conversation with one another so that we can figure out what matters to us," she said. "It should be what matters to every elected official."

She wanted the attendees to take their ideas home and spread the enthusiasm to their friends. After a couple of hours of brainstorming in small groups, each group presented its ideas to snaps of approval from fellow attendees. They suggested the youth vote could be increased by providing a bus to transport people to polling locations in states where citizens can register on Election Day; asking YouTube stars to integrate voting explainers into their video content; and building a website to match people with a "buddy" in their city so each could hold the other accountable for going to the polls.

One group brought up perhaps the most practical solution of all: build a more informed young voting pool by improving civics education and bringing registration information to eighteen- and soon-to-be eighteen-year-olds where they're most easily found: high school.

FIRST VOTE!

Aerial Towles, eighteen, marched with her dad following the Nashville Party at the Polls. She held a hot pink sign that read, "Engage Connect Empower." It wasn't just any walk for Towles—she was heading toward her first vote. "I'm extremely excited," Towles said. "I'm really inspired by all the sacrifices that have been made for me to be able to vote." The stories she heard growing up about her own grandfather's voting struggle as an African American made the moment particularly special.

GO WHERE THE KIDS ARE

While high schools are an obvious place to register young voters, it's far from standard for high school students to be walked through the registration process and taught the details of voting. That's true even in the states (and the District of Columbia) that allow sixteen- and seventeen-year-olds to preregister so their registration is automatically active when they turn eighteen.

As with all things in voting, some states are better than others in encouraging schools to register voters. Various nonpartisan organizations large and small are trying to fill the education gaps and crack the code of registering would-be voters as early as possible. One focus is promoting peer-to-peer registration—training high schoolers to help register their classmates.

Since 2014, Inspire2Vote (formerly known as Inspire U.S.) has done that very job in states including Arizona, Colorado, Kentucky, and Virginia, with plans to expand as the 2020 election nears. Inspire works with groups that already have contacts in the community to identify students and teachers or administrators who would be receptive to the training. The hope is students will pass down the voter registration project from year to year, with the leadership moving from student to student like student council positions.

VOTING TIP:

Learn about how voting can make a difference and create change around you by participating in your school's student government. Consider running for something!

YOUNG LEADER FOCUS: ANDAYA SUGAYAN

Andaya Sugayan graduated from college in 2017 and now works with Inspire and other civics-related charities as a one-woman organization, Inspire PA. She's always in her car, driving between high schools in and around Pittsburgh and Philadelphia to register young voters, providing more voting pledge cards when classes have run out, and answering questions via text about elections from students and teachers alike.

Sugayan, who grew up near Seattle, is high energy and organized. She credits her high school government teacher with inspiring her by holding mock elections and even having members of political campaigns visit the school to pitch their plans.

So Sugayan was delighted last fall when a school she visited to help register students also held their student council elections on the same day; local election officials brought new voting machines for the students to use.

Sugayan's style of get-out-the-vote work can be found in the bios of many successful public servants. In her book *Becoming*, Michelle Obama describes how Barack Obama was asked to run the Illinois chapter of a non-partisan voter registration organization when he was in his early thirties. "To say that Barack threw himself into the job would be an understatement. The goal of Project VOTE! was to sign up new Illinois voters at a staggering pace of ten thousand per week," she wrote, adding that the hardest people to reach were—you guessed it—the eighteen- to thirty-year-olds.

Young people are often accused of not caring about voting. But those who work with high schoolers find it to be more of a case of not having yet learned to connect voting with its impact on their lives.

REGISTERING FELLOW STUDENTS

At many Inspire school visits, students ask a lot of questions. It makes it "very obvious that we are the very first people talking to the students about the voting process," Inspire's Mixdorf said. They discuss both how to register and vote and what politics mean in students' everyday lives by focusing on issues like how school board decisions affect school facilities and extracurricular activities.

MAKING VOTING A GAME

Making registration a team sport of sorts has also proven to be an effective tool in the success of peer-to-peer registration.

- Student leaders at a West Virginia high school registered 100 percent of their eligible student body and then helped start a voting program at their rival school. Both schools bussed students to the polls for the 2018 primary elections. Also on the bus? A middle-aged teacher who registered with her students and was also voting for the first time.

- A Southern California high school registered or preregistered 630 students. A rival high school said they could do better, and bested them by more than 100 registrants.

- Multiple secretary of state offices have gotten in on the competition vibe, giving awards to schools that do a particularly good job registering students.

The Civics Center launched in California in September 2018, and had helped with high school voter registration drives in at least twenty-five states just a year later. The organization provides a step-by-step guide for holding a drive, and suggests reaching out to local organizations, like the League of Women Voters, to help out.

The Civics Center sends teachers a "Democracy in a Box" kit, including stickers and streamers to celebrate the drive, a clipboard with a planning worksheet and state-specific information, like voter ID requirements, plus posters to publicize the event. The box also includes candy in a "Democracy in a Bag" tote.

Schools need training and support, the Civics Center founder Laura Brill said, but the true power comes from the students. Student-driven events allow administrators to relax about any concerns of partisanship from outside groups. "When it's the kids wanting what's fundamentally an educational experience about civics and voting, it's very authentic," Brill said.

VOTING TIP:

The Civics Center has a way for students to participate even if they're not old enough to preregister: students are encouraged to list three friends or family members they promise to get to vote. You are never too young to encourage those around you to vote!

Here are some suggestions if you're taking an adult to the polls:

THE DAY BEFORE

- Ask them to help you figure out when you'll be eligible to vote. Some states allow sixteen- and seventeen-year-olds to preregister, and even vote in primaries if they'll be eighteen by Election Day.
- Ask them about the first time they voted and why voting is important to them.
- Together, find news articles about the election and talk about the races on the local ballot.
- Discuss differences between the candidates' views.
- Ask if they'll need an ID to vote, and what kind.
- Voting lines are sometimes long. Pack a book or activity to help pass the time.
- Check the weather. Will you need an umbrella? Sunglasses? A coat?
- Voters often get an "I Voted" sticker specific to their city. Look up your local one. (Some places even have "future voter" stickers!)

VOTING DAY

- At check-in, pay attention to what the poll workers are asking—they're confirming your adult is registered and in the right place.

- If you have a question, ask the poll worker. They are there to help.
- Notice everyone gets privacy to vote—a vote is a personal choice.
- If it's a paper ballot, make sure your adult is filling in the ovals fully and neatly.
- With the poll worker's permission, ask if you can drop the ballot into the box or feed it into the machine.
- Don't forget the sticker!

THAT NIGHT OR THE NEXT DAY

- Check election results and discuss who won and lost, and by how much.
- Tell your friends all about your voting adventure.

Some of these tips may need to be modified if your adult votes by mail, but the idea is the same—ask to participate and ask a lot of questions. You'll be on your way to being a voter.

POSITIVE PEER PRESSURE

Michelle Obama's nonpartisan When We All Vote organization is trying to get newly eligible voters and previous nonvoters to the polls through a mix of education, community outreach, and friendly peer pressure. Obama is able to harness major star power—the group's debut announcement included Lin-Manuel Miranda (the genius behind the musical *Hamilton*), basketball player Chris Paul, singer Janelle Monáe, actor Tom Hanks, and country music stars Faith Hill and Tim McGraw. But among the most important things they did, according to Kyle Lierman, the CEO of When We All Vote, was establish a hashtag that would encourage everyone—from rapper Cardi B to Iowa teenagers—to vote and to bring their friends along.

Obama herself kicked it off, asking people to choose five friends or family members to be in their #VotingSquad, and then to make sure each voted. "You are the best messengers to get out the vote. You know who's too busy or too forgetful or who might flake out on election day. . . . Tag each other on Instagram and Facebook . . . put everyone on a text chain, and then get to the polls," she said. It resulted in a seemingly endless scroll on social media of selfies of people's #VotingSquad, including winter-hat-wearing ladies in Oregon, parents escorting their twin daughters to cast their first votes, and women spelling out VOTE in yoga positions.

One of the organization's first priorities was to focus on people in zip codes with low registration rates and recruit volunteers in those communities to host registration events during the group's "Week of Action." They're expanding their squad idea into 2020, asking people to sign up to be "Squad Captains." Duties include choosing people to join your voting squad and signing up for a monthly call with When We All Vote for updates and suggestions on getting out the vote. When primary elections were postponed or altered due to the coronavirus pandemic, the group kept people up-to-date on social media on the status of the elections and options to vote by mail.

MEETING PEOPLE WHERE THEY ARE: NONPROFIT VOTE

Another group of Americans who vote at low rates are those who come from households that make the least money. An organization called Nonprofit VOTE worked with community health centers, food pantries, housing associations, and other organizations across the country to ask their clients to register or pledge to vote. When they followed up after the 2018 midterm elections, they found that the clients they spoke to were more likely to vote than others in their income level.

YOU'RE NEVER TOO YOUNG TO PARTICIPATE

Even if preregistration is a few years away for you, you can still consider participating in learning about issues and encouraging others to vote.

• Ask a parent, or another adult close to you, to check into get-out-the-vote efforts in your area, and see if you can join them or help them get organized.

- Ask a parent or other adult close to you if they plan on canvassing—going door-to-door to promote a candidate, party, or issue. Ask if you can join them.

- Find out if there's a voter registration drive happening at your local high school. If you're in middle school, see if your student government can assist the high school effort by making signs or getting the word out.

- Think about issues you care about—animal rights? Immigration? College debt? Ask an adult to help you find out what your options are to become educated and to start contributing to the change you're hoping to see.

MAKING VOTING PERSONAL

erhaps no get-out-the-vote movement has felt more personal than that of the "Parkland kids." After the horrific shooting on their high school campus, the students and alumni of Marjory Stoneman Douglas High School founded March for Our Lives and oversaw its voter recruitment efforts, determined to make a difference.

Several March for Our Lives members traveled to Nashville to emcee the 2018 event where Sheryl Crow was performing—a pre-midterm morning concert and voting party organized by a fellow Parkland alumnus. Sitting around a table backstage, they described how they told people that the best way to make their feelings known to public officials is to vote.

If someone thinks voting isn't worth it or is too much trouble, March for Our Lives members know what to do. "Sometimes it's just as easy as making a plan with someone," said Brendan Duff, a 2016 graduate of Stoneman Douglas. "They don't know where their polling place is, they don't know [poll] hours . . . But if you go through it with them and show them the resources and walk them through a solid, tangible process, they're much more likely to actually vote."

WHO WAS MARJORY STONEMAN DOUGLAS?

The woman their high school was named after—Marjory Stoneman Douglas—would surely be impressed with their efforts. President Bill Clinton gave her the Presidential Medal of Freedom in 1993 for her environmental activism. But when she was a young woman in her twenties, she had another cause—fighting for the women's suffrage amendment to make sure all U.S. women could vote. Douglas was 108 years old when she died in 1998.

Several of the Parkland kids wore white sweatshirts with an American flag, but in place of the square of stars was a QR code that could be scanned with a smartphone to lead directly to voter registration sites. They'd done an organized "shirt drop" at more than a thousand schools and colleges, said Matt Deitsch, the organization's chief strategist and another Stoneman alumnus.

The youngest people at the table that day in Nashville, Kirsten McConnell, a Parkland senior, and Daniel Duff, Brendan's younger brother, were quiet for most of the discussion. But when asked if they had anything to add, Daniel, several years shy of voting age, laughed a little, and joined the chorus of others sharing a single message: Vote!

MOTIVATING THEIR OWN TEAM OF VOTERS

Barack Obama administration alums are in the get-out-the-vote game in a way that's specific for their own team. Former speechwriters Jon Favreau and Jon Lovett and former National Security Council spokesman Tommy Vietor founded a company called Crooked Media in 2017. They're best known for *Pod Save America*, a podcast that reached its first million-listener episode shortly after its launch.

It covers the news from a politically left-leaning perspective and frequently welcomes Democratic candidates and commentators. Their goal was to avoid jargon—language about a topic that's difficult to understand for those who don't know about the topic—and instead to talk about politics like real people do.

Talking about the details of voting and explaining voter suppression have been a top priority for the company. They regularly encourage podcast listeners to visit their Vote Save America site to register or confirm their registration.

YOUNG LEADER FOCUS: SHANIQUA MCCLENDON

Shaniqua McClendon graduated from college in 2009 and later attended Harvard's Kennedy School of Government. Her dream job was to work at a media company with some names people would know so she could use that power to increase civic engagement. She found it when she became Crooked Media's first political director.

McClendon has an early memory that made her understand the importance of speaking up for those who can't speak up for themselves. She was in first grade and asked her teacher, "Can I go to the bathroom?" Her teacher said, "I don't know, can you?" (The teacher wanted her to say, "May I go to the bathroom?") The confused first grader put her hand down and sat quietly, but she also wet her pants. McClendon remembers a friend being kind to her, and her mom having some strong words for the teacher about being more understanding. McClendon never forgot feeling voiceless and helpless, and wants to help others who might feel that way.

Going into 2020, Vote Save America partnered with a left-leaning organization called Fair Fight 2020 to raise money for voter education and to fight voter suppression. They raised more than $1 million from listeners in two weeks. McClendon celebrated the fundraising victory on Instagram, pouring jelly beans into a container marked with numbers to show the amount raised.

In 2018, Crooked Media asked listeners to volunteer to help get out the vote, and connected the volunteers to campaigns in need. They signed people up for 23,000 volunteer shifts for Democratic candidates across the country, a number that felt low to McClendon until she remembered they'd had only about two months to do it. Like those sharing their When We All Vote squad, voters and volunteers used #votesaveamerica to share their experience and encourage others to join in voting and volunteering. Before the November 2019 elections, Vote Save America reminded followers on Instagram to post their volunteer efforts, saying, "Peer Pressure! Sometimes it's good."

POLITICAL JARGON: CANVASSING

Canvassing: going door-to-door to remind voters to vote, or ask them to vote for a specific candidate or issue.

A taped segment on their HBO show featured Vietor, Lovett, and comedienne Akilah Hughes knocking on doors in a neighborhood and asking people if they planned to vote. The video's tone was a mix of silly humor and seriousness. "Canvassing doesn't just turn out the people you talk to. The other people in that home are also 60 percent more likely to vote," Lovett said, adding people should put their phones down, stop tweeting, and hit the pavement to canvass. "Because it's the single best thing you can do."

Volunteerism was the touchstone for Swing Left, another left-leaning organization that threw its energies into recruiting volunteers to work for races where the Republican representative didn't have a big lead. Swing Left wanted to switch certain House of Representatives seats held by Republicans to being Democratic ones. The group helped people find their closest volunteer opportunity.

On a Thursday night in Manhattan, the last before the 2018 midterm elections, a line snaked around Cooper Union's Great Hall as Swing Left volunteers waited to get into the building where Abraham Lincoln and Elizabeth

Cady Stanton both once spoke (separately, of course).

Backstage was twenty-one-year-old Zoe Petrak, a Fordham University student. She was camera-ready in a white V-neck T-shirt and black leather jacket, ready to take the stage with Mark Ruffalo, the *Avengers* actor: "The 2016 election was the first election I was eligible to vote in," she told the crowd, but afterward she'd wished she'd found more ways to participate. "I didn't do enough! I just voted."

When her classmates would tell her their one vote wouldn't make a big enough difference, Petrak explained volunteering was a way to give their one vote more power. "If you go out and talk to people . . . that's how you make your vote matter more," she said.

POLITICAL JARGON: PARTY TICKET

When someone is said to vote a **"party ticket,"** it means they are voting for people from the same political party on all the races on the ballot.

The name comes from the time when the government didn't print the ballots and people had to bring their own. Political parties would hand out ballots ahead of time that looked like train tickets—that's where the "party tickets" name comes from—so voters could use them even if they couldn't read or write.

The government-issued ballots as we now know them are an import from Australia. In 1888, Massachusetts became the first state in the nation to pass a law requiring the Australian ballot.

What seems reasonable now was a discrimination tool then; the paper ballot supplied by the government kept those who couldn't read from participating.

FUN FACTS

Not all states took up paper ballots right away. Kentucky voted by voice until 1891!

The point of highlighting the work of organizations like these is not to tell you how to vote. It's to show how some of the large, coordinated efforts are working not just to get out the vote, but to educate others and spread the voting message.

The most successful voter drives involve making the message personal, whether it's knocking on doors, recruiting your friends, or reminding your parents to make their plan to vote.

STUDYING VOTERS: WHAT GETS THEM TO THE POLLS?

Do you sometimes get a sticker when you go to the doctor or do well on a school report? It turns out adults sometimes get stickers, too. And they love it!

Adults get an "I Voted" sticker when they cast their ballot, and usually the sticker has a picture that shows something about their city or state. If you check social media on Election Day, you'll find all sorts of people showing off their stickers. Some people even put them on their pets.

I VOTED!

New York City's "I Voted" sticker used to have colorful intersecting lines that looked like the city's subway map, but it changed in 2019 to the New York City sky-line. Las Vegas's also features the Statue of Liberty and the Empire State Building, along with the Eiffel Tower and Great Pyramid, all recognizable replica landmarks on that city's horizon. "I Voted" appears on a California sticker in thirteen languages, including Thai and Tagalog. Some Tennessee voters get one in the shape of their state, while the sticker of its southern neighbor is dominated by a pretty Georgia peach.

WHEN DID THE "I VOTED" STICKER START?

Time magazine cites 1992 as the likely first media mention of the "I Voted" sticker, when the *Miami Herald* reported Florida businesses were offering discounts to customers wearing theirs. Miami-Dade made sticker news again more than thirty years later with a story about voting stickers getting a "multicultural makeover." The sticker included "I voted!" in three languages (English, Spanish, Creole), complete with the hashtag #iamelectionready.

Stickers have even been used to encourage people to vote early. Alaska's usual sticker is modeled after its state flag's blue-with-yellow-stars constellation. But people who voted early in Alaska for the 2018 elections got special stickers drawn by an Alaskan artist. The stickers showed animals doing Alaska-ish things, including a walrus on a snowmobile and a moose in a lumberjack-style red-checked shirt. Those who waited to vote until Election Day would have only the old blue-and-yellow sticker to show for it.

According to the *Anchorage Daily News*, there were more 2018 early voters than the total number of early voters in the last three similar Alaskan elections. Could it be that voters braved the long early voting lines for the sticker? Was it just part of record-breaking early voting turnout nationwide? Trying to figure that out is one of the things social scientists who study elections do.

VOTER ENCOURAGEMENT TACTICS

Experts spend a lot of time trying to learn what makes a person show up to vote. Columbia University professor Donald Green and Alan Gerber of Yale University wrote *Get Out the Vote!: How to Increase Voter Turnout*, the go-to adult book on encouraging voter turnout. In it they describe experimental research on voter encouragement tactics to see if they increase turnout. Some examples of what they found:

- Robocalls, where a recorded voice tells you about an election or candidate, have basically no effect. They're annoying and easy to ignore.
- Canvassing, where people go door-to-door to speak to

voters, does work. But beware a volunteer so passionate about their candidate they can't listen to the person they're visiting.

- What about including a voting storyline in a Spanish-language soap opera to increase voter registration among Latinx? Sounds fun, but results in a small increase, at best.

SOCIAL PRESSURE

Get Out the Vote goes on to describe "social pressure" communications as playing on "a basic human drive to win praise and avoid chastisement." People like to be praised and dislike being criticized. With voting, the praise comes from casting a ballot and the criticism from failing to meet one's responsibility.

Who someone votes for is private; whether or not they voted is public information. Research found that the type of "social pressure" that resulted in the greatest increase in a person's likelihood of voting was mail to people's homes that talked about whether or not the people who lived there had voted in recent elections, as well as if people in their neighborhood had. It was a big breakthrough on what might make a difference in voter turnout!

But there was a problem. People thought it was creepy to get mail telling them someone looked up whether they voted, and especially to compare them to their neighbors. A Wisconsin organization that used the "Neighbors" version received hundreds of complaints. Ever since, campaigns and voting advocates have been trying to find a happy medium of reminding people to vote, and that their voting record is public, without making them angry!

One note: people are less worried about being outed as nonvoters if campaigns contact them by phone. Texts were less effective, and sometimes not effective at all.

THANK-YOU NOTES FOR VOTES

One option avoids the risks of social pressure but still garners benefits—Green described it as a kind of early thank-you note. These flatter the recipient about voting in the past in hopes it'll encourage them to vote the next time, too. The thank-you notes are the kinder, gentler way of saying, "Yep, we're watching."

Even just thanking people for voting without talking about their past history can increase turnout. It's an option with little or no downside for campaigns or get-out-the-vote groups. Most people like being appreciated for doing their civic duty. Especially if they get a sticker!

"I AM A VOTER"

Some get-out-the-vote methods move beyond encouraging you to pat yourself on the back. Research says that certain language used right before an election—asking someone if they'll "be a voter" rather than just if they'll "vote"—can increase the chance the person will vote. It has to do with how you think of yourself. A "voter" becomes a good thing that a person *is*, rather than voting being something they only *do*.

While other researchers disagreed that such a language trick works, I like the idea of making voting so much of a habit, and something that you think so important, that it feels like part of who you are.

Thinking of yourself as a voter echoes what

organizations like When We All Vote, Inspire, and We Vote Next are trying to do. They're showing that voting is something Americans should think about as an ongoing part of our lives, not something to consider only every four years.

A STRAIGHTFORWARD, WELCOMING MESSAGE

That idea and the "be a voter" research both came to mind when I saw pictures from a New York fashion show by designer Prabal Gurung. The seat assignments were printed on a white card with a simple phrase in black letters: "I am a voter." Within weeks, basketball superstar Stephen Curry was holding up to the camera a small black pin with the same phrase.

Using language to think about voting as part of personal identity, like someone labeling herself an entrepreneur, film buff, or foodie, inspired the "I am a voter" campaign, said creator and cofounder Mandana Dayani. Dayani was born in Iran, and a refugee organization helped resettle her family in America when she was a young girl. She became a corporate lawyer, and later served as the vice president of fashion company Rachel Zoe. After the 2016 election she wanted to be involved in getting more people to vote.

She realized what she thought was missing: a voting

brand that appealed to younger adults, one that wasn't preachy but was welcoming and cool. In spring 2018, she asked her friend Tiffany Bensley, who helped shape marketing for luxury brands, and about a dozen other creative women to join her in finding a way to make people want to go to the polls at every opportunity. Natalie Tran, an executive at entertainment and talent giant Creative Artists Agency's foundation, is also a cofounder, and CAA helped provide the organization with logistical and financial support to spread their message.

They selected a simple font and decided on a clear and forceful period at the end. "That's so much more powerful because you're now declaring a statement about yourself," Dayani said.

They stayed away from the stereotypical reds, blues, and waving flags of most political messaging in favor of a sleek black-and-white look. They included in the @iamavoter Instagram stories selfies of people who tagged a picture of themselves wearing one of their T-shirts, hoodies, or pins.

A lot of companies were willing to help spread the message. Star Wars director J. J. Abrams's production company was one of them. For a month, AMC Theatres showed an announcement before movies that ended with the "I am a voter" logo and a number to text for registration and voting information. The fashion website Who What Wear was among several companies that participated in a "digital shutdown" asking people to take a break from Instagram and register to vote. (Digital shutdowns have become a tool many companies, individuals, and websites use to encourage voter registration.)

The campaign focused on positive and powerful language and facts about voting, rather than using shaming language about low voter turnout rates.

They've registered voters at gatherings as diverse as the extravaganza that is the Beautycon cosmetics convention (famously described as "Sephora meets Coachella") and at WE Day UN, a youth empowerment day held during the meeting of the United Nations General Assembly. Shortly after National Voter Registration Day last year, Curry invited the "I am a voter" team to help register his Golden State Warrior teammates.

ATHLETES AND VOTING

RISE to Vote is an organization that works with coaches and players of both professional and college teams to spread the word about the importance of voting and how to register.

RISE held registration sessions with teams including the NFL's Atlanta Falcons and the NBA's San Antonio Spurs, as well as some Major League Baseball teams and more than twenty college athletic programs. The organization also held events at the Super Bowl and NBA All-Star Game, and at the NCAA Final Four, where basketball fans could walk through a timeline of sports and social activism, "interview" players in a mock dressing room—and then register to vote.

YOUNG LEADER FOCUS: MADISON ROBERTS

The registration sessions work best when it's the players who encourage their teammates to join. In 2018, University of California–Berkeley lacrosse player Madison Roberts helped register her teammates, and then arranged time with other Berkeley coaches to talk to their teams as well. Roberts told radio station WBUR that she's a "world-class hair braider," and started telling friends she wouldn't braid their hair unless they registered to vote. Her mom said it made sense—when Roberts was a little girl, she'd ask to go into the voting booth, would pull the voting lever, and even get her own "I voted" sticker.

MAKE IT A PARTY

Parties work.

"This is very much part of American [voting] tradition," said Professor Green of Columbia, even if it's something people have forgotten over time. Before reforms in the 1880s sought to protect voters from undue influence and bribery, election days were freewheeling events where voters hung out for hours, eating, drinking alcohol, and enjoying entertainment. That party-like atmosphere could go very wrong—1800s elections also saw fights, threats to voters, and even riots. Luckily, there are ways to adopt the fun without the bad behavior and danger.

Green and fellow researchers looked at how family-friendly festivals can influence turnout. Experiments involved choosing neighboring towns with similar numbers of people and voting rates, and in one of them holding a town party on Election Day with cotton candy, music, raffles, and the like. The other towns were left festival-free. In one New Hampshire example, an "Election Day Poll Party" was advertised and received press coverage, and perfect spring weather resulted in increased turnout. (Weather matters in a party's turnout success.)

#VOTETOGETHER

In the lead-up to the 2016 election, Green worked with a nonprofit group to test the theory on even bigger festivals—there was more local outreach and a variety of entertainment at the different sites, including dancers, photo booths, and even puppies. Looking at nine festivals, they saw a turnout of nearly 4 percent higher than comparable non-party cities. In close elections, 4 percent can change the whole race.

The effort, which became known as #VoteTogether, expanded in 2018 with more than 1,900 parties held in all fifty states. The general idea is for local organizations or chapters of nonpartisan organizations like the YMCA, the United Way, and the NAACP to organize an event tailored to their community. #VoteTogether (which provides a toolkit with all the dos and don'ts) suggests the community parties be held in viewing distance of a polling place on Election Day, and that some type of food, music, and entertainment is provided. In 2018 that meant everything from a few tables with pizza to a local DJ playing music to a party with live musicians performing for hundreds.

Shira Miller, who oversees the #VoteTogether effort (it's now under the umbrella of Civic Advisors, which works with Obama's When We All Vote), said the goal is for the celebrations to become a habit. "We are working to change the culture around voting by making it community-driven . . . to try to make participation in Election Day just as celebratory as participating in the Fourth of July," she said.

YOU MATTER

Think of every Election Day as a chance to celebrate Americans' right to vote—even before you can vote yourself—by encouraging adults around you to go to the polls!

A wealth of organizations are here to help, but in the

end, it really all does come down to you.

Your vote is your voice. Use it as soon as you can! And until then, use your actual voice, your texting fingers, your Instagram images, and any other social media you've got to encourage the people you know and love to vote. You—not a politician, not a celebrity, not an athlete, but you—are the greatest inspiration to your family, your friends, your classmates, and your online community.

From me to you, sincerely: thank you for voting.

THANK YOU FOR VOTING:
TELL YOUR FRIENDS

Choose five people you're going to make sure vote. Tag them below (the old-fashioned way—write it down!) and, if you have a social media account, post a picture of your list and tag them there, too. Include **@thankyouforvoting** on Instagram.

Dear

@ _____

@ _____

@ _____

@ _____

@ _____

Let's make our voices heard on Election Day. Will you promise to vote? I'll check in to make sure you do. Thank you for voting!

@ _____

FOR MORE INFORMATION

To find out more information about voting as well as organizations you can participate in, here are some websites to visit.

- League of Women Voters: www.lwv.org
- Vote 411: www.vote411.org
- March for Our Lives: marchforourlives.com
- We Vote Next: www.eighteenx18.com
- When We All Vote: www.whenweallvote.org
- Rock the Vote: www.rockthevote.org
- USA.gov: www.usa.gov/register-to-vote
- Inspire2Vote: www.inspire2vote.org
- The Civics Center: thecivicscenter.org

ACKNOWLEDGMENTS

Thank you to Karen Chaplin for wanting to make a young readers' edition of *Thank You for Voting* and caring so much about it reaching a new audience. Thank you to Kathleen Krull for making the book more kid friendly, and to Laura Mock for designing the cover and the Brave Union for the illustrations. Thank you to the entire team at Harper Kids who got this book to the finish line.

Thank you to Dan Kirschen at ICM for helping me navigate this new world.

Thank you to all the teachers who fostered my love of reading, took time to encourage my writing, and provided me with tips I use daily, especially:

My all-time favorite teacher: Debbie Randel (also known as my mom!)

Elementary school: Roxie Madding, Linda Barton

Middle school: Sherry Brackin, Mary Partlow, Rick Schultz

High school: Laurie Vaught, Beverly Davis, Bruce Wright

College: Marvin Olasky, Mercedes De-Uriarte

Law school: Sarah Cleveland, Bill Powers

Journalism school: John Bennet, Stephen Fried, Paula Span

Thank you to Bryan for endless support through the writing of both editions.

And to Reed: Thank you for being you and for being so excited about this book. And, when the time comes, for using your kind and brilliant voice to support democracy.

SOURCE NOTES

NOTE TO THE READER

2 *"the only way they could do that is by not voting"*:
Franklin D. Roosevelt, "The Great Communicator," The
Master Speech Files, 1898, 1910–1945, File No. 1539, October 5,
1944, http://www.fdrlibrary.marist.edu/_resources/images/msf
/msfb0170.

4 *Reported Voter Turnout Rate by Age*: "Voting in
America: A Look at the 2016 Presidential Election," Census
.gov, Census Blogs, May 10, 2017, https://www.census.gov
/newsroom/blogs/random-samplings/2017/05/voting_in_
america.html.

8 *The Importance of Farmers*: Domenico Montanaro,
"Why Do We Vote on Tuesdays," NPR.org, November 1, 2016,
https://www.npr.org/2016/11/01/500208500/why-do-we-vote-on
-tuesdays.

CHAPTER 1: STRUGGLING FOR VOTING EQUALITY

13 *The First Democracy*: "Democracy (Ancient Greece)," *National Geographic*, Encyclopedic Entry, https://www .nationalgeographic.org/encyclopedia/democracy-ancient-greece/.

14 *"New claims will arise"*: John Adams to James Sullivan, May 26, 1776, National Archives, Founders Online, https:// founders.archives.gov/documents/Adams/06-04-02-0091.

16 *the first vote took place in 1789*: "First U.S. Presidential Election," History.com, https://www.history.com/this-day-in -history/first-u-s-presidential-election.

17 *George Washington received* all *the electoral votes*: "Presidential Election of 1789," The Fred W. Smith National Library for the Study of George Washington at Mount Vernon, mountvernon.org, https://www.mountvernon.org /library/digitalhistory/digital-encyclopedia/article/presidential -election-of-1789/.

CHAPTER 2: AFRICAN AMERICANS AND THE VOTE

20 *he left him a lot of money*: "Robert Purvis," National Park Service, https://www.nps.gov/people/robert-purvis.htm.

20 *Pennsylvania Abolition Society*: "Robert Purvis," History Society of Pennsylvania, http://digitalhistory.hsp.org /pafrm/person/robert-purvis.

20 *"Appeal of Forty Thousand Citizens, Threatened with Disfranchisement"*: Robert Purvis, "Appeal of Forty Thousand Citizens, Threatened with Disfranchisement," http:// digitalhistory.hsp.org/pafrm/doc/appeal.

20 *African Americans from Tennessee*: Black Residents of Nashville to the Union Convention of Tennessee (1865), http://www.freedmen.umd.edu/tenncon.htm.

22 *"Black enthusiasm for political participation"*:

Alexander Keyssar, *The Right to Vote* (New York: Basic Books, 2000), 73.

23 *South Carolina's state legislature*: Blain Roberts and Ethan Kytle, "When the South Was the Most Progressive Region in America," *The Atlantic*, January 17, 2018, https://www.theatlantic.com/politics/archive/2018/01/when-the-south-was-the-most-progressive-region-in-america/550442/.

24 *didn't protect voting rights as some lawmakers wanted*: Keyssar, *The Right to Vote*, 74, 81.

26 *"became shorthand"*: Becky Little, "Who Was Jim Crow?," *National Geographic*, August 6, 2015, https://www.nationalgeographic.com/news/2015/08/150806-voting-rights-act-anniversary-jim-crow-segregation-discrimination-racism-history/.

26 *in the correct box*: Darryl Paulson, "Florida's History of Suppressing Blacks' Votes," *Tampa Bay Times*, October 11, 2013, https://www.tampabay.com/news/perspective/floridas-history-of-suppressing-blacks-votes/2146546/.

26 *turnout in the state dropped from 62 percent to 11 percent*: Michael J. Klarman, *From Jim Crow to Civil Rights: The Supreme Court and the Struggle for Racial Equality* (New York: Oxford University Press, 2004), 32.

26 *decreased to around 5,300*: James Bryce, *The American Commonwealth*, vol. 2, 3rd ed. (New York: Macmillan, 1897), 545, https://books.google.com/books/about/The_American_Commonwealth_The_party_syst.html?id=5K7ff2MCKBwC.

26 *By 1940, only 3 percent*: "Voting Rights Act: Major Dates in History," ACLU, https://www.aclu.org/voting-rights-act-major-dates-history.

28 *Student Nonviolent Coordinating Committee*: Ari Berman, *Give Us the Ballot* (New York: Picador, 2015), 4–5.

28 *a toothbrush, and two books*: Berman, *Give Us the Ballot*, 5.

29 *"Many of the issues of civil rights"*: Lyndon Baines Johnson, "Special Message to Congress," LBJ Presidential Library, Speeches and Films, March 15, 1965, http://www.lbjlibrary.org/lyndon-baines-johnson/speeches-films/president-johnsons-special-message-to-the-congress-the-american-promise.

29 *250,000 African Americans*: "Voting Rights Act: Major Dates in History," ACLU, https://www.aclu.org/voting-rights-act-major-dates-history.

29 *59.8 percent after*: U.S. Commission on Civil Rights, "The Voting Rights Act: Ten Years After," January 1975, p. 43, https://lccn.loc.gov/75601086.

30 *"been like that in the first place"*: Berman, *Give Us the Ballot*, 42.

CHAPTER 3: NATIVE AMERICANS AND THE VOTE

33 *they could take power*: Daniel McCool, Susan M. Olson, and Jennifer L. Robinson, *Native Vote* (Cambridge: Cambridge University Press, 2007), 3–4.

34 *"Indians not taxed"*: McCool, *Native Vote*, 12.

34 *Bill Clinton's administration*: Andrew Oxford, "It's Been 70 Years Since Court Ruled Native Americans Could Vote in New Mexico," *Santa Fe New Mexican*, August 2, 2018, https://www.santafenewmexican.com/news/local_news/it-s-been-years-since-court-ruled-native-americans-could/article_d0544a48-ef37-56ef-958f-eb81dcf01344.html.

35 *Western state elections in the 1950s*: McCool, *Native Vote*, 20.

35 *repealed the law the next year*: McCool, *Native Vote*, 96–97.

CHAPTER 4: IMMIGRANTS AND THE VOTE

37 *But a mere twenty-five years*: Keyssar, *The Right to Vote*, 27.

37 *before they became citizens*: Keyssar, *The Right to Vote*, 65.

38 *"I know nothing"*: Lorraine Boissoneault, "How the 19th-Century Know Nothing Party Reshaped American Politics," Smithsonian.com, January 26, 2017, https://www.smithsonianmag.com/history/immigrants-conspiracies-and-secret-society-launched-american-nativism-180961915/.

38 *bar natives of China from voting*: Keyssar, *The Right to Vote*, 114.

39 *Chinese immigrants given the opportunity*: "Timeline of Chinese Immigration to the United States," The Bancroft Library, University of Californi,a Berkeley, https://bancroft.berkeley.edu/collections/chinese-immigration-to-the-united-states-1884-1944/timeline.html.

39 *Japanese and other Asian immigrants*: "Asian American History," Japanese American Citizens League, https://jacl.org/asian-american-history/.

39 *half of eligible Asian Americans did*: Jens Manuel Krogstad and Mark Hugo Lopez, "Black Voter Turnout Fell in 2016, Even as a Record Number of Americans Cast a Ballot," Pew Research Center, May 12, 2017, https://www.pewresearch.org/fact-tank/2017/05/12/black-voter-turnout-fell-in-2016-even

-as-a-record-number-of-americans-cast-ballots/.

39 *higher than the 2014 election*: William H. Frey, "2018 Turnout Rose Dramatically for Groups Favoring Democrats, Census Confirms," Brookings, May 2, 2019, https://www .brookings.edu/research/2018-voter-turnout-rose-dramatically -for-groups-favoring-democrats-census-confirms/.

CHAPTER 5: EIGHTEEN-YEAR-OLDS AND THE VOTE

41 *to make sure the VRA extension passed*: Keyssar, *The Right to Vote*, 225–27.

41 *lower the voting age only for federal elections*: *Oregon v. Mitchell*, U.S. Supreme Court, 400 U.S. 112 (1970), https:// supreme.justia.com/cases/federal/us/400/112/.

CHAPTER 6: SUFFERING FOR WOMEN'S SUFFRAGE

44 *"repeal our Masculine systems"*: John Adams to Abigail Adams, letter, April 14, 1776, Adams Family Papers, Massachusetts Historical Society, https://www.masshist.org /digitaladams/archive/doc?id=L17760414ja&hi=1&query =Intimation%20that%20another%20Tribe&tag=text&archive =letters&rec=2&start=0&numRecs=329.

45 *school-related issues*: "Kentucky and the 19th Amendment," National Park Service, https://www.nps.gov /articles/kentucky-and-the-19th-amendment.htm.

45 *shouldn't women have them, too*: Sally Roesch Wagner, *The Women's Suffrage Movement* (New York: Penguin Books, 2019), 45.

45 *women's rights convention was born*: Wagner, *The Women's Suffrage Movement*, 57–58.

46 *"Civil and Political Rights of Women"*: Notice of

Women's Rights Convention, *Seneca County Courier*, July 14, 1848, Library of Congress, available at https://www.loc.gov /resource/rbnawsa.n7548/?st=text.

46 *convention's "Declaration of Sentiments"*: Liz Robbins and Sam Roberts, "Early Feminists Issued a Declaration of Independence. Where Is It Now?," *New York Times*, February 9, 2019, https://www.nytimes.com/interactive/2019/02/09 /nyregion/declaration-of-sentiments-and-resolution-feminism .html; Valerie Jablow, "Tea and Sisterhood," Smithsonian.com, October 1998, https://www.smithsonianmag.com/history/tea -and-sisterhood-158244677/.

46 *Frederick Douglass*: Ta-Nehisi Coates, "Frederick Douglass: 'A Women's Rights Man,'" *The Atlantic*, September 30, 2011.

48 *eloquently about women's rights*: Angela P. Dodson, *Remember the Ladies* (New York: Center Street/Hachette, 2017), 141–44.

48 *"but it is comin'"*: Proceedings of the Woman's Rights Convention, September 6 and 7 (New York: Fowler and Wells, 1853), https://cdn.loc.gov/service/rbc/rbnawsa/n8289/n8289.pdf.

48 *Their formal organization*: Lori D. Ginzberg, *Elizabeth Cady Stanton: An American Life* (New York: Hill and Wang, 2009), 108–09.

49 *"the Negro's hour"*: Dodson, *Remember the Ladies*, 191.

49 *"ballot equal to our own"*: Mark Leibovich, "Rights vs. Rights: An Improbable Collision Course," *New York Times*, January 13, 2008, https://www.nytimes.com/2008/01/13 /weekinreview/13leibovich.html.

50 *American Woman Suffrage Association*: Allison

Lange, *"Suffragists Organize: American Woman Suffrage Association,"* National Women's History Museum, http://www .crusadeforthevote.org/awsa-organize.

51 *wanted the vote for white women*: Dodson, *Remember the Ladies*, 249.

51 *upsetting for Southerners*: Dodson, *Remember the Ladies*, 256.

51 *telling his wife about the events of the day*: Frederick Douglass obituary, *New York Times*, February 20, 1895, https://www.nytimes.com/2019/02/14/obituaries/frederick -douglass-dead-1895.html.

52 *so the sculptor added Truth*: Nicole Brown, "Sojourner Truth Added to Proposed Women's Suffrage Monument in Central Park," *AM New York*, https://www.amny.com/news /sojourner-truth-statue-1-34951402/.

53 *170 meetings*: Susan B. Anthony, diary entry, January 1, 1872, Susan B. Anthony Papers, Library of Congress, https:// www.loc.gov/exhibitions/women-fight-for-the-vote/about-this -exhibition/seneca-falls-and-building-a-movement -1776–1890 /a-movement-at-odds-with-itself/relentless-travel-and-a-new -departure/.

53 *"little band of nine ladies"*: "Minor Topics," *New York Times*, November 6, 1872, https://timesmachine.nytimes.com /timesmachine/1872/11/06/issue.html.

54 *encourage women to move there*: Mary Schons, "Woman Suffrage," *National Geographic*, January 21, 2011, https://www.nationalgeographic.org/news/woman-suffrage/.

54 *suffrage organizations in most counties*: "Utah and the 19th Amendment," National Park Service, https://www.nps .gov/articles/utah-women-s-history.htm.

55 *"We want our beer"*: Dawn Langan Teele, "How the West Was Won: Competition, Mobilization, and Women's Enfranchisement in the United States," *Journal of Politics* 80, no. 2 (April 2018): 447.

55 *"we won't have it"*: Carrie Chapman Catt and Nettie Rogers Shuler, *Woman Suffrage and Politics* (New York: Charles Scribner's Sons, 1923), 89.

57 *against racial discrimination*: Keyssar, *The Right to Vote*, 164–65.

57 *Britain's suffrage movement*: Dodson, *Remember the Ladies*, 277.

58 *never took to it in the same way*: Katie Steinmetz, "Everything You Need to Know about the Word 'Suffragette,'" *Time*, October 22, 2015, https://time.com/4079176/suffragette-word-history-film/.

58 *Iowa and California*: "Youngest parader in New York City Suffrage Parade," Shall Not Be Denied: Women fight for the vote, Library of Congress, loc.gov/resource/cph.3g05585/.

58 *"sixty years of hard struggle"*: "Miss Susan B. Anthony Died This Morning," *New York Times*, March 13, 1906, https://timesmachine.nytimes.com/timesmachine/1906/03/13/101769455.html?pageNumber=1.

58 *"moved by seeing marching groups"*: Harriot Stanton Blatch, "Why Suffragists Will Parade on Saturday," *New York Tribune*, May 3, 1912, https://chroniclingamerica.loc.gov/lccn/sn83030214/1912-05-03/ed-1/seq-1/.

59 *Suffrage Doll*: Janice Ruth, interview with author, May 30, 2019.

59 *negative things about the movement*: Elizabeth Cobbs, "Op-Ed: Woodrow Wilson's Woman Problem, a Case Study

for the Trump Era," *Washington Post*, January 18, 2017, https://
www.latimes.com/opinion/op-ed/la-oe-cobbs-wilson-womens
-march-20170118-story.html.

60 *women's suffrage supporters marching*: John Kelly,
"Long Before Pink Hats, Female Protesters Marched in D.C.
for Women's Rights," *Washington Post*, March 13, 2018,
https://www.washingtonpost.com/local/long-before-pink-hats
-female-protesters-marched-in-dc-for-womens-rights/2018/03/13
/4b1335f2-26be-11e8-874b-d517e912f125_story.html.

60 *"they made it their own"*: Ruth, interview with author,
May 30, 2019.

61 *"can afford a little while to wait"*: Woodrow Wilson,
"Address at the Women's Suffrage Convention, Atlantic City,
N.J., September 8, 1916," President Wilson's State Papers
and Addresses, 327, https://books.google.com/books?id=u2su
AAAAIAAJ&pg=PA327&lpg=PA327#v-onepage&q&f-false.

61 *"we want it to come during your administration"*: Ida
Husted Harper, ed., *National American Woman Suffrage
Association's The History of Woman Suffrage, Volume V:
1900–1920, After Seventy Years Came the Victory* (New York:
J. J. Little & Ives Company, 1922), 488–99.

62 *the vote instead of jail sentences*: "Suffragists Wire
Wilson," *New York Times*, July 19, 1917, https://timesmachine
.nytimes.com/timesmachine/1917/07/19/96257621.html?page
Number=2.

62 *three-hour procession*: Dodson, *Remember the Ladies*,
308.

64 *"some bunch of guys"*: Cokie Roberts, "100 Years Ago
This Week, House Passes Bill Advancing 19th Amendment,"
interview by Steve Inskeep, NPR, May 22, 2019, https://www

.npr.org/2019/05/22/725610789/100-years-ago-this-week-house
-passes-bill-advancing-19th-amendment.

65 *told they couldn't vote*: Jen Rice, "How Texas
Prevented Black Women from Voting Decades After the 19th
Amendment," Houston Public Media, June 28, 2019, https://
www.houstonpublicmedia.org/articles/news/in-depth/2019/06
/28/338050/100-years-ago-with-womens-suffrage-black-women
-in-texas-didnt-get-the-right-to-vote/.

65 *every presidential election since*: "Gender Differences
in Voter Turnout," Center for American Women and Politics,
Rutgers University, https://www.cawp.rutgers.edu/sites
/default/files/resources/genderdiff.pdf.

CHAPTER 7: VOTING PROBLEMS AND VOTING SOLUTIONS

66 *a 2017 Pew study*: "Public Supports Aim of Making It
'Easy' for All Citizens to Vote," Pew Research Center, June 28,
2017, https://www.people-press.org/2017/06/28/public-supports
-aim-of-making-it-easy-for-all-citizens-to-vote/.

66 *61 percent*: "Voting in America: A Look at the 2016
Presidential Election," Census.gov, Census Blogs, May 10,
2017, https://www.census.gov/newsroom/blogs/random
-samplings/2017/05/voting_in_america.html.

66 *2018*: "Voter Turnout Rates Among All Voting Age and
Major Racial and Ethnic Groups Were Higher than in 2014,"
Census.gov, Census Blogs, April 23, 2019, https://www.census
.gov/library/stories/2019/04/behind-2018-united-states-midterm
-election-turnout.html.

68 *"None of you would be here"*: Jeremy Bird, interview
with author, March 16, 2018.

70 *"varying election laws of the different States"*: James

Bryce, *The American Commonwealth*, vol. 2, 3rd ed. (New York: Macmillan, 1897), 142, https://books.google.com/books /about/The_American_Commonwealth_The_party_syst .html?id=5K7ff2MCKBwC.

70 *mailing ballots to all eligible voters*: "Voting Outside the Polling Place: Absentee, All-Mail and Other Voting at Home Options," National Conference of State Legislatures, February 20, 2020, https://www.ncsl.org/research/elections -and-campaigns/absentee-and-early-voting.aspx.

71 *begin their preparations*: Craig Timberg, "Voting By Mail, Already on the Rise, May Get a $500 Million Federal Boost from Coronavirus Fears," *Washington Post*, March 10, 2020, https://www.washingtonpost.com/technology/2020/03/10 /mail-voting-coronavirus-bill/.

72 *successful voter drives targeting African Americans*: Jonathan Mattise, Associated Press, and Elaina Sauber, *The Tennessean*, "Federal Judge Blocks Tennessee Voter Registration Law, Citing Harm to 'Constitutional Rights,'" *The Tennessean*, September 12, 2019, https://www.tennessean.com /story/news/2019/09/12/tennessee-voter-registration-law -blocked-judge-citing-harm/2300293001/.

72 *prior felony conviction*: Jean Chung, "Felony Disenfranchisement: A Primer," The Sentencing Project, June 27, 2019, https://www.sentencingproject.org/publications/felony -disenfranchisement-a-primer/.

CHAPTER 8: VOTER SUPPRESSION AND FIGHTING AGAINST IT

75 *"a locked door right in front of you"*: Mimi Marziani, interview with author, April 16, 2019.

76 *Andrew Young*: Berman, *Give Us the Ballot*, 95–98.

76 *a fifty-year-old teacher*: Berman, *Give Us the Ballot*, 138–39.

76 *Shelby County*: Adam Liptak, "Supreme Court Invalidates Key Part of Voting Rights Act," *New York Times*, June 25, 2013, https://www.nytimes.com/2013/06/26/us/supreme-court-ruling.html.

77 *Right away*: Ed Pilkington, "Texas Rushes Ahead with Voter ID Law After Supreme Court Decision, *The Guardian*, June 25, 2013, https://www.theguardian.com/world/2013/jun/25/texas-voter-id-supreme-court-decision; and Michelle Miller, Phil Hirschkorn, "Voter ID Bill Raises Controversy in North Carolina," CBSNews.com, August 13, 2013, https://www.cbsnews.com/news/voter-id-bill-raises-controversy-in-north-carolina/.

77 *struck down*: Camila Domonoske, "Supreme Court Declines Republican Bid to Revive North Carolina Voter ID Law," NPR, May 15, 2017, https://www.npr.org/sections/thetwo-way/2017/05/15/528457693/supreme-court-declines-republican-bid-to-revive-north-carolina-voter-id-law.

77 *"Voter suppression is tricky"*: Celina Stewart and Jeanette Senecal, interview with author, March 27, 2019.

78 *"cornerstone of our democracy"*: "Voting Rights: What's at Stake," ACLU.org. https://www.aclu.org/issues/voting-rights.

79 *ACLU's voting rights division*: Dale Ho, interview with author, July 23, 2018.

79 *more difficult to vote*: "Election 2012: Voting Laws Round-up," Brennan Center for Justice, October 11, 2012, https://www.brennancenter.org/our-work/research-reports/election-2012-voting-laws-roundup.

80 *cull their lists*: *Husted v. A. Philip Randolph Institute*, U.S. Supreme Court, 584 U.S. __ (2018), https://supreme.justia.com/cases/federal/us/584/16-980/.

81 *"notice from election officials"*: Adam Liptak, "Supreme Court Upholds Ohio's Purge of Voting Rolls," *New York Times*, June 11, 2018, https://www.nytimes.com/2018/06/11/us/politics/supreme-court-upholds-ohios-purge-of-voting-rolls.html.

82 *five actually cast a ballot*: Jessica Huseman, "How the Case for Voter Fraud Was Tested—and Utterly Failed," ProPublica, June 19, 2018, https://www.propublica.org/article/kris-kobach-voter-fraud-kansas-trial.

CHAPTER 9: THE PRESENT AND FUTURE OF VOTING

83 *too much focus on suppression*: Senecal, interview with author, March 27, 2019.

84 *Top Questions of Voters*: Senecal, interview with author, March 27, 2019.

85 *electoral behavior and voting laws*: Paul Gronke, interview with author, March 6, 2019.

85 *benefits were notable*: Rob Griffin, Paul Gronke, Tova Wang, and Liz Kennedy, "Who Votes with Automatic Voter Registration?," Center for American Progress, June 7, 2017, https://www.americanprogress.org/issues/democracy/reports/2017/06/07/433677/votes-automatic-voter-registration/.

86 *one million new voters registered*: *Times* Editorial Board, "Despite Bungled Debut of 'Motor Voter' Law, It's Delivering New Voters as Promised," *Los Angeles Times*, April 15, 2019, https://www.latimes.com/opinion/editorials/la-ed-motor-voter-dmv-20190415-story.html.

87 *improved everywhere AVR was used*: Kevin Morris and Peter Dunphy, "AVR Impact on State Voter Registration," Brennan Center for Justice, April 11, 2019, https://www.brennancenter.org/our-work/research-reports/avr-impact-state-voter-registration.

87 *Registration, of course, doesn't guarantee voting*: Nathaniel Rakich, "What Happened When 2.2 Million People Were Automatically Registered to Vote," FiveThirtyEight, October 10, 2019, https://fivethirtyeight.com/features/what-happened-when-2-2-million-people-were-automatically-registered-to-vote/.

88 *registered that same day*: "Election Administration and Campaigns," Office of the Minnesota Secretary of State Steve Simon, https://www.sos.state.mn.us/election-administration-campaigns/data-maps/historical-voter-turnout-statistics/.

88 *"It's easy for voters to understand"*: Celina Stewart and Jeanette Senecal, interview with author, March 27, 2019.

88 *"We could spend that money"*: Jeremy Bird, interview with author, March 16, 2018.

90 *Maine became the first*: Steve Mistler, "Future of Maine's Ranked-Choice Voting Experiment at Stake in Tuesday's Election," Maine Public Radio, June 12, 2018, https://www.mainepublic.org/post/future-maines-ranked-choice-voting-experiment-stake-tuesdays-election.

CHAPTER 10: WHAT IS GERRYMANDERING?

96 *can predict voter behavior*: Vann R. Newkirk II, "How Redistricting Became a Technological Arms Race," *The*

Atlantic, October 28, 2017, https://www.theatlantic.com
/politics/archive/2017/10/gerrymandering-technology-redmap
-2020/543888/.

97 *expert in U.S. House of Representatives politics*:
David Wasserman, interview with author, May 16, 2019.

98 *three out of thirteen congressional seats*: Thomas
Wolf and Peter Miller, "How Gerrymandering Kept Democrats
from Winning Even More Seats Tuesday," *Washington Post*,
November 8, 2018, https://www.washingtonpost.com/outlook
/2018/11/08/how-gerrymandering-kept-democrats-winning
-even-more-seats-tuesday/.

99 *Hoverboard behind Peppa Pig*: David Daley, *Ratf**ked*
(New York: Liveright Publishing Corporation), 2017.

99 *Fajita Strip*: Kevin Diaz, "Texas Gerrymandering Case
before Supreme Court Could Change State's Political Map,"
Houston Chronicle, April 20, 2018, https://www.houstonchronicle
.com/news/politics/texas/article/Gerrymandering-case-could
-change-the-political-12851565.php#.

99 *Broken-Winged Pterodactyl*: Editorial Board, "Time for
Maryland to Get Rid of 'Broken-winged Pterodactyl' Electoral
Districts," *Washington Post*, January 27, 2016.

100 *electing a candidate of their own choice*: *Thornburg
v. Gingles*, U.S. Supreme Court, 478 U.S. 30 (1986), https://
supreme.justia.com/cases/federal/us/478/30/#tab-opinion
-1956757.

101 *took away the one district in Maryland*: *Lamone v.
Benisek*, U.S. Supreme Court, Case No. 18–726 (2019), https://
www.oyez.org/cases/2018/18-726.

102 *fairly drawn district*: *Rucho v. Common Cause*, U.S.

Supreme Court, Case No. 18–422, Brief for Appellees, League of Women Voters of North Carolina, 1.

102 *"political task of districting to political actors"*: *Rucho v. Common Cause*, U.S. Supreme Court, Case No. 18–422, Brief for Appellants, 7, https://www.supremecourt.gov/Docket PDF/18/18-422/92363/20190319113346714_18-422%20rb.pdf.

103 *how much partisanship*: *Rucho v. Common Cause*, U.S. Supreme Court, Case No. 18–422, 2019, Brief for Appellants, 11.

103 *a majority of the court*: *Rucho v. Common Cause*, U.S. Supreme Court, 588 U.S. ___ (2019), June 27, 2019, opinion, https://supreme.justia.com/cases/federal/us/588/18-422/#tab -opinion-4114540; dissent, https://supreme.justia.com/cases /federal/us/588/18-422/#tab-opinion-4114540.

105 *gerrymandering was partly to blame*: Katie Fahey, interview with author, April 25, 2019.

107 *Tribeca Film Festival*: Owen Gleiberman, "Tribeca Film Review: 'Slay the Dragon,'" *Variety*, April 28, 2019, https:// variety.com/2019/film/reviews/slay-the-dragon-review -gerrymandering-1203199856/.

CHAPTER 11: THE NEWS: YOUR SUPERPOWER

109 *"incredible information literally available at our fingertips"*: Alan Miller, interview with author, April 16, 2019.

109 *"It's open at all hours"*: Brian Stelter, interview with author, April 24, 2019.

110 *the types of information*: "Info Zones," Checkology .org, https://get.checkology.org/lesson/infozones/.

110 *Raw Information*: "Raw Information Needs Context for

Healthy Consumption," The News Literacy Project (News Lit Tips), https://newslit.org/get-smart/raw-information-needs-context/.

112 *Propaganda*: John Silva, "Distinguishing among news, opinion, and propaganda," News Literacy Project, June 20, 2018, https://newslit.org/educators/civic-blog/distinguishing-among-news-opinion-and-propaganda/.

116 *"standards, biases, or beliefs"*: Michael Schmidt, interview with author, November 26, 2018.

119 *"nothing more embarrassing"*: Stelter, interview with author, April 24, 2019.

122 *the better you are at telling fact from opinion*: Amy Mitchell, Jeffrey Gottfried, Michael Barthel, and Nami Sumida, "Distinguishing Between Factual and Opinion Statements in the News," Pew Research Center, June 18, 2018, https://www.journalism.org/2018/06/18/distinguishing-between-factual-and-opinion-statements-in-the-news/.

122 *false information found its way*: Craig Silverman et al., "Hyperpartisan Facebook Pages Are Publishing False and Misleading Information at an Alarming Rate," BuzzFeed News, October 20, 2016, https://www.buzzfeednews.com/article/craigsilverman/partisan-fb-pages-analysis#.tom4Bwyro.

CHAPTER 12: UNDERSTANDING POLLING

130 *spoonful of soup*: Philip Bump, interview with author, June 16, 2019.

133 *"margin of error"*: Andrew Mercer, "5 Key Things to Know About the Margin of Error in Election Polls," Pew Research Center, September 6, 2016, https://www.pewresearch

.org/fact-tank/2016/09/08/understanding-the-margin-of-error-in
-election-polls/.

137 *on the minds of the American people*: Karlyn
Bowman, interview with author, May 2, 2019.

137 *Americans' top concerns over time*: Gregor Aisch and
Alicia Parlapiano, "What Do You Think Is the Most Important
Problem Facing This Country Today?," *New York Times*,
February 27, 2017, https://www.nytimes.com/interactive/2017
/02/27/us/politics/most-important-problem-gallup-polling
-question.html.

138 *government/poor leadership*: "Most Important
Problem," Gallup, https://news.gallup.com/poll/1675/most
-important-problem.aspx.

139 *big report of their findings*: "An Evaluation of 2016
Election Polls in the U.S.," Ad Hoc Committee on 2016 Election
Polling, American Association for Public Opinion Research,
May 4, 2017, https://www.aapor.org/Education-Resources
/Reports/An-Evaluation-of-2016-Election-Polls-in-the-U-S.aspx.

CHAPTER 13: WHAT ABOUT THE ELECTORAL COLLEGE?

141 *unique among democracies*: Drew DeSilver, "Among
Democracies, U.S. Stands Out in How It Chooses Its Head of
State," Pew Research Center, November 22, 2016, https://www
.pewresearch.org/fact-tank/2016/11/22/among-democracies-u-s
-stands-out-in-how-it-chooses-its-head-of-state/.

145 *Electors are like "mirrors"*: Sanford Levinson,
interview with author, May 8, 2019.

146 *"role of kingmaker"*: Norman J. Ornstein, "Three
Disputed Elections: 1800, 1824, 1876," in *After the People Vote:*

A Guide to the Electoral College, ed. John C. Fortier, 3rd ed. (Washington, DC: The AEI Press, 2004), chap. 7.

149 *a compelling reason*: Alexander Keyssar, interview with author, May 21, 2019; Garrett Epps, "The Electoral College Was There from the Start," *The Atlantic*, September 8, 2019, https://www.theatlantic.com/ideas/archive/2019/09/electoral-college-terrible/597589/.

149–50 *keep founders from slaveholding states happy*: Sean Wilentz, "The Electoral College Was Not a Pro-Slavery Ploy," *New York Times*, April 4, 2019, https://www.nytimes.com/2019/04/06/opinion/electoral-college-slavery.html; Akhil Reed Amar, "Actually the Electoral College Was a Pro-Slavery Ploy," *New York Times*, April 6, 2019, https://www.nytimes.com/2019/04/06/opinion/electoral-college-slavery.html.

150 *"particular weird institution"*: Alexander Keyssar, interview with author, May 21, 2019.

151 *there was silence*: Patrick Svitek, Bobby Blanchard, and Aliyya Swaby, "Texas Electors Cast 36 Votes for Trump, 1 for Kasich and 1 for Ron Paul," *Texas Tribune* (video available), December 19, 2016, https://www.texastribune.org/2016/12/19/watch-texas-electoral-college-vote-begins-texas-ca/.

151 *Republican elector Art Sisneros*: Michael Marks, "This Texas Elector Resigned Rather Than Voting for Donald Trump," KUT.org, November 29, 2016, https://www.kut.org/post/texas-elector-resigned-rather-voting-donald-trump.

151 *78 percent of the vote in Liberty County*: "2016 Texas Presidential Election Results," Politico.com, December 31, 2016, https://www.politico.com/2016-election/results/map/president/texas/.

153 *700 proposals*: "Past Attempts at Reform," FairVote, https://www.fairvote.org/past_attempts_at_reform.

154 *stolen from dead soldiers and shot his own mother*: Ornstein, "Three Disputed Elections: 1800, 1824, 1876."

154 *believed until his dying day*: Ornstein, "Three Disputed Elections: 1800, 1824, 1876."

155 *population numbers don't alone warrant*: Levinson, interview with author, May 8, 2019.

156 *combined 196 Electoral College votes*: Caroline Kelly, "Oregon Governor Signs Bill Granting State's Electoral Votes to National Popular Vote Winner," CNN.com, June 12, 2019, https://www.cnn.com/2019/06/12/politics/oregon-joins-national -popular-vote-compact/index.html.

156 *untested system*: John Fortier, interview with author, April 24, 2019.

CHAPTER 14: YOUNG PEOPLE AND VOTING

163 *similar to what it's been since 1974*: "Youth Voting Historically," Center for Information & Research on Civic Learning and Engagement (CIRCLE), https://civicyouth.org /quick-facts/youth-voting/.

163 *The jump from 2014 to 2018*: "Voter Turnout Rates Among All Voting Age and Major Racial and Ethnic Groups Were Higher Than in 2014," Census.gov, https://www.census .gov/library/stories/2019/04/behind-2018-united-states-midterm -election-turnout.html.

164 *Rock the Vote campaign*: "About Us," Rock the Vote, https://www.rockthevote.org/about-us/#ourhistory.

165 *"we're at a turning point"*: Sheryl Crow, interview with author, October 20, 2018.

165 *Disliking the candidates and issues*: "Why Youth Don't Vote—Differences by Race and Education," CIRCLE, August 21, 2018, https://civicyouth.org/why-youth-dont-vote -differences-by-race-and-education/.

166 *six years before*: "Harvard IOP youth poll finds stricter gun laws," Harvard Kennedy School Institute of Politics, June 18, 2018, https://iop.harvard.edu/about/newsletter-press-release /harvard-iop-youth-poll-finds-stricter-gun-laws-ban-assault -weapons.

166 *"Because I vote all the time and you don't"*: Paul Gronke, interview with author, March 6, 2019.

167 *"Imagine the power"*: Hannah Mixdorf, interview with author, October 1, 2019.

CHAPTER 15: SPEAKING YOUR LANGUAGE

170 *Among them was a young woman*: We Vote Next Summit, "Voting Class of 2018," https://static1.squarespace .com/static/5a5fbce0d55b412c123047c3/t/5c070aba352f53d9bcd8 1889/1543965371297/2018+DELEGATE+YEARBOOK.pdf.

172 *Aerial Towles, eighteen, marched with her dad*: Aerial Towles, interview with author, October 20, 2018.

173 *Inspire2Vote*: Hannah Mixdorf, Chelsea Costello, Olivia McCuskey of Inspire U.S. and Inspire2Vote (Inspire), interviews with author, January 23, June 26, and October 1, 2019.

173 *moving from student to student*: Hanna Mixdorf, interview with author, October 1, 2019; Laura Brill of the Civics Center, interview with author, October 1, 2019.

173 *She's always in her car*: Andaya Sugayan, interview

with author, September 27, 2019.

174 *"To say that Barack threw himself into the job"*: Michelle Obama, *Becoming* (New York: Crown Publishing Group, 2018), 166–67.

175 *a middle-aged teacher*: Chelsea Costello (Inspire), interview with author, January 23, 2019.

175 *A rival high school said they could do better*: Brill, interview with author, October 1, 2019.

176 *voter registration drives in at least twenty-five states*: Brill, interview with author, October 1, 2019.

179 *a hashtag that would encourage everyone*: Kyle Lierman, interview with author, March 27, 2019.

179 *"then get to the polls"*: Michelle Obama, "Create your VotingSquad," When We All Vote, October 26, 2018, https://action.whenweallvote.org/page/s/create-your-voting-squad.

180 *Squad Captains*: "Voting Squad Starter Guide," when we all vote, whenweallvote.org/wp-content/uploads/2020/01/WWAVVOTING/SquadGuide-01172020.pdf.

180 *more likely to vote than others in their income level*: Brian Miller, Caitlin Donnelly, and Caroline Mak, "Engaging New Voters," Nonprofit VOTE, May 1, 2019, https://www.nonprofitvote.org/documents/2019/05/engaging-new-voters-2018.pdf/.

CHAPTER 16: MAKING VOTING PERSONAL

182 *a table backstage*: March for Our Lives members, interview with author, October 20, 2018.

183 *Marjory Stoneman Douglas*: Marjory Stoneman Douglas, National Women's Hall of Fame, https://www

.womenofthehall.org/inductee/marjory-stoneman-douglas/.

184 *shortly after its launch*: Jason Zengerle, "The Voices in Blue America's Head," *New York Times Magazine*, November 22, 2017, https://www.nytimes.com/2017/11/22/magazine/the -voices-in-blue-americas-head.html.

186 *asked listeners to volunteer*: Shaniqua McClendon, interview with author, February 26, 2019.

187 *"single best thing you can do"*: "Canvassing," *Pod Save America*, October 13, 2018, https://www.youtube.com /watch?v=GwghDw48iu0.

187 *Swing Left wanted to switch*: Sridhar Pappu, "Trying to Flip the House, Zip Code by Zip Code," *New York Times*, July 20, 2018, https://www.nytimes.com/2018/07/20/business /swing-left-primary-campaigns.html.

188 *"how you make your vote matter more"*: Adrienne Lever and Zoe Petrak, interview with author, November 1, 2018.

188 *"party tickets"*: Jill Lepore, "Rock, Paper, Scissors," *New Yorker*, October 6, 2008, https://www.newyorker.com /magazine/2008/10/13/rock-paper-scissors.

188 *"import from Australia"*: Jill Lepore, "Rock, Paper, Scissors."

188 *Massachusetts became the first state*: Lepore, "Rock, Paper, Scissors."

CHAPTER 17: STUDYING VOTERS: WHAT GETS THEM TO THE POLLS?

190 *"I Voted"*: Olivia B. Waxman, "This Is the Story Behind Your 'I Voted' Sticker," *Time*, November 6, 2018, https:// time.com/4541760/i-voted-sticker-history-origins/.

191 *Miami-Dade made sticker news*: Douglas Hanks, "For Miami-Dade, a New 'I Voted' Sticker," *Miami Herald*, January 29, 2016, https://www.miamiherald.com/news/local/community /miami-dade/article57277743.html.

191 *special stickers drawn by an Alaskan artist*: Adelyn Baxter, "Vote Early to Get One of Juneau Artist Pat Race's 'I Voted' Stickers," Alaska Public Media, KTOO—Juneau, October 23, 2018, https://www.alaskapublic.org/2018/10/23/vote -early-to-get-one-of-juneau-artist-pat-races-i-voted-stickers/.

192 *more 2018 early voters*: Tegan Hanlon, "'It's Really Popular': Early Voting Numbers Are Up in Alaska Compared to Previous Elections for Governor," *Anchorage Daily News*, November 3, 2018.

192 *go-to adult book on encouraging voter turnout*: Donald P. Green and Alan S. Gerber, *"Get Out the Vote: How to Increase Voter Turnout*," 4th ed. (Washington, D.C.: Brookings Institution Press, 2019).

192 *Robocalls*: Green and Gerber, "Commercial Phone Banks, Volunteer Phone Banks, and Robocalls," in *Get Out the Vote!*, chap. 6.

192 *Canvassing*: Green and Gerber, "Door-to-Door Canvassing," in *Get Out the Vote!*, chap. 3.

193 *Spanish-language soap opera*: Green and Gerber, "Using Mass Media to Mobilize Voters," in *Get Out the Vote*, chap. 9.

193 *"social pressure" communications*: Green and Gerber, "Strategies for Effective Messaging," in *Get Out the Vote*, chap. 11.

194 *less worried about being outed*: Green and Gerber,

"Electronic Mail, Social Media, and Text Messaging," in *Get Out the Vote!*, chap. 7.

194 *early thank-you note*: Donald Green, interview with author, April 12, 2018.

194 *people like being appreciated*: Green and Gerber, "Strategies for Effective Messaging," in *Get out the Vote*, chap. 11.

CHAPTER 18: "I AM A VOTER"

195 *"be a voter"*: Christopher J. Bryan, Gregory M. Walton, Todd Rogers, and Carol S. Dweck, "Motivating Voter Turnout by Invoking the Self," Proceedings of the National Academy of Sciences 108, no. 31 (2011): 12653–12656, https://cpb-us-w2 .wpmucdn.com/voices.uchicago.edu/dist/b/232/files/2016/09 /Motivating-voter-turnout-by-invoking-the-self-118b75n.pdf.

195 *other researchers disagreed*: Alan S. Gerber, Gregory A. Huber, Daniel R. Biggers, and David J. Hendry, "A Field Experiment Shows that Subtle Linguistic Cues Might Not Affect Voter Behavior," Proceedings of the National Academy of Sciences, June 28, 2016, https://www.pnas.org /content/113/26/7112; Alan Gerber, Gregory Huber, Albert Fang, "Do Subtle Linguistic Interventions Priming a Social Identity as a Voter Have Outsized Effects on Voter Turnout? Evidence from a New Replication Experiment: Outsized Turnout Effects of Subtle Linguistic Cues," *Political Psychology* 39, no. 4 (August 2018): 925–38.

196 *inspired the "I am a voter" campaign*: Mandana Dayani, interview with author, April 4, 2019.

198 *"Sephora meets Coachella"*: Elizabeth Holmes,

"Beauty Is in the Eye of These Beholders," *New York Times*, July 28, 2018.

199 *Madison Roberts*: Matthew Stock, "How One College Athlete is Getting Out the Vote," WBUR.org, https://www .wbur.org/onlyagame/2018/11/02/madison-roberts-college -athlete-voter-registration-cal.

199 *"part of American [voting] tradition"*: Donald Green, interview with author, April 12, 2018.

199 *election days were freewheeling events*: Green and Gerber, "Using Events to Draw Voters to the Polls," in *Get Out the Vote!*, chap. 8.

200 *how family-friendly festivals can influence turnout*: Green and Gerber, "Using Events to Draw Voters to the Polls," *Get Out the Vote!*, chap. 8.

201 *live musicians performing for hundreds*: Shira Miller, interview with author, September 19, 2019.